About the Author

KT-499-889

JOHN SCOTNEY M.A., RSA, was the BBC's Head of Drama in Ireland and later Head of the BBC TV Drama Script Unit. A graduate of the University of Cambridge, he has written books and articles about literature and the media, and written and directed numerous programs for the BBC, many on Irish themes, including a critically acclaimed version of James Joyce's *Ulysses*. He is a former advisor to the Arts Council, university lecturer, and was Chair of the Writers' Guild of Great Britain, Deputy Chair of the National Poetry Society, and is a Fellow of the Royal Society of Arts. For Kuperard he has also written *Culture Smart! Scotland* and *The Theory of Evolution*.

The Culture Smart! series is continuing to expand.
For further information and latest titles visit
www.culturesmart.co.uk

The publishers would like to thank **CultureSmart!**Consulting for its help in researching and developing the concept for this series.

CultureSmart!Consulting creates tailor-made seminars and consultancy programs to meet a wide range of corporate, public-sector, and individual needs. Whether delivering courses on multicultural team building in the USA, preparing Chinese engineers for a posting in Europe, training call-center staff in India, or raising the awareness of police forces to the needs of diverse ethnic communities, it provides essential, practical, and powerful skills worldwide to an increasingly international workforce.

For details, visit www.culturesmartconsulting.com

CultureSmart!Consulting and **CultureSmart!** guides have both contributed to and featured regularly in the weekly travel program "Fast Track" on BBC World TV.

contents

contents

Map of Ireland

introduction

This is a book about Ireland and its people, not "the Irish" in the broadest sense. Visitors from the crowded cities of America, from densely populated mainland Europe, and from even more densely populated Japan are often delighted by how empty Ireland seems, with its broad countryside, little towns, and uncongested roads. Northern Ireland is three times as densely peopled as the Republic, yet even so the whole island is home to to fewer than six and three-quarter million people.

But "the Irish" worldwide is a different matter! In the USA forty million citizens are of Irish stock; 15 percent of the population of New Zealand, 14 percent of Canadians and 30 percent of Australians have Irish forebears. Argentina has an ethnic Irish population of around 300,000, and Irishmen played major roles in the development of South America. Bernard O'Higgins, Captain General of Chile, Grand Marshal and Captain General of Peru, General of Grand Colombia etc., etc., is counted among the *Libertadores*, the heroes of South America's struggle for independence. And in Britain there are more than a million people born in Ireland, and perhaps five million of Irish descent.

What this colossal exodus means to the Irish, how it came about, and how the population of Ireland fell from eight million in 1840, is something you will need to know if you are to understand modern Ireland. But there is a lot more to this remarkable island that has peopled the world with men and women who still remain loyal to their origins, and that has given so much in the way of music, drama, and literature. Ireland has had an influence, and endured a history, out of all proportion to its size, and it has done so because of its people.

Most guidebooks tell you where to stay and what to see. This series is written for people who want to know more and go deeper. Here you will find the beliefs and attitudes of the Irish, their rich musical and literary culture, their ancient language and mythology, the values they live by, how they do business, how they enjoy themselves, the way they have been molded by their history and indeed by geography. This understanding will be appreciated by your hosts; it will open doors to you, even open the hearts of a generous, talented people, justifiably proud of their unique identity.

Key Facts – The Republic of Ireland

Ireland is a single geographical entity—an island off the western coast of Europe. It is home to two political units, one an independent self-governing republic, Eire (pronounced "AIR-uh'"), often called "the Republic," to distinguish it from Northern Ireland, which is part of the United Kingdom with some elements of self-government.

Official Name	Eire, or Ireland	Article 4 of the Republic's 1937 constitution states "The name of the state is Eire or in the English language, Ireland."
Capital City	Dublin	
Main Cities	Dublin, Cork, Galway, Limerick	
Area	About 27,000 square miles (70,000 sq. km). Eire occupies 85% of the island of Ireland, all except the northeastern corner.	
Climate	Temperate	
Population	About 4.9 million. Well over a million in Dublin. 60% of the population live in urban areas, mostly within 50 miles (100 km) of Dublin. Growth rate: 1.77% per annum	
Currency	The Euro (€1 = 1.4 US dollars)	
Ethnic Mix	85% native Irish. 2.7% Polish, 2.5% UK born, increasing Indo/Pakistani community, and small Jewish and Chinese minorities	
Family Size	5% of families have over 4 children	Average number of children per woman: 1.4
Language	Two official languages: Gaelic and English. Gaelic is studied in schools, but only 77,000 people use it in daily life (they also speak English). Many Gaelic words appear in public life.	
Religion	About 85% officially Roman Catholic; 6% have no religion, and the rest are mainly Anglican.	

Government	Parliament, called the *Oireachtas*, has two chambers: the Senate, *Seanad Eireann*, and the house of representatives, the *Dail Eireann*. The head of state is the President, elected for seven years. Real power lies with the *Taioseach*, or Prime Minister.
Local Government Structure	Eire is divided into 26 counties. Ancient Ireland was made up of four provinces, formerly kingdoms: Ulster, Munster, Leinster, and Connaught. Ulster is now mainly in Northern Ireland.
Legal System	The heads of the legal system are the judges of the Supreme Court, appointed by the President on the advice of the Prime Minister and cabinet. The legal system is based on English Common Law, but much modified by the Constitution and by laws and judgments made since independence.
Cost of Living	Currently the cost of living is much the same as in the United Kingdom.
Ports and Airports	Dublin and Cork are the main ports, Dublin and Shannon the main airports.
Media	*Raidió Teilifís Éireann*, the national broadcasting body, has two English television channels: RTE1 and Network 2, and an Irish-language channel TG4. The independent commercial station is TV3. BBC and other UK channels are available in much of the country as are Northern Irish transmissions.	*Raidió Teilifís Éireann* has the five main radio channels: Radio 1 (Speech & Music), Radio 1 Extra (speech), 2FM (popular culture), Lyric FM (classical music), *Raidió na Gaeltachta* (Irish Language channel). There are 2 national commercial and numerous local radio stations.
	Several English-language newspapers, notably the *Irish Times*, are also available daily on the Web.

Electricity	The Irish electrical system operates on 220–240 volts, 50 Hz	Sockets and plugs as in the UK. Visitors from continental Europe will need adapters. Americans will need adapters both for the voltage cycles and plugs and sockets.
Internet Domain	.ie	
Telephone	The international code for Ireland is 00 353.	Telecommunications are highly advanced.
Time	Greenwich Mean Time	The same as for the United Kingdom

Key Facts – Northern Ireland

Official Name	Province of Northern Ireland	The Province is sometimes called Ulster, but actually includes only six of the original nine counties of the kingdom of Ulster.
Capital	Belfast	
Main Cities	Belfast, Londonderry, Omagh	
Area	5,500 square miles (14,000 sq. km)	
Climate	Temperate	
Population	1.8 million. Mostly in the east, where Belfast has a population of over 280,000.	
Currency	Pound Sterling. English notes and coins are legal tender, as are the notes issued by Scottish banks. Additionally four Northern Irish banks issue their own notes. (£1 = US $1.50)	

Ethnic Mix	89% Northern Irish, many with Scottish forebears. Small Indian and larger Polish and Chinese communities	
Family Size	Average number of children per woman: 2.0	
Language	English	
Religion	42% Protestant, 41% Catholic; the rest mostly no religion	
Government	Northern Ireland is part of the United Kingdom and elects 18 members to the British Parliament, but has its own Assembly at Stormont with limited legislative and administrative powers.	
Legal System	As in the UK, with some modifications, notably under the Prevention of Terrorism Act 1974	
Cost of Living	Noticeably lower than elsewhere in the UK	
Media	Closely linked to those in the rest of the UK, and also overlaps with print, television, and radio in the Republic. Two publicly funded television channels, BBC 1 and BBC 2 with local content, as well as BBC4. The Commercial station is ITV Ulster. In addition digital channels are available from Eire and the rest of the UK.	The five UK-wide BBC radio stations, as well as the three UK-wide commercial radio services (Classic FM, Talk Sport, and Virgin Radio) are also available. Two national radio stations: BBC Radio Ulster, operated by the BBC, and the commercial Downtown Radio, as well as several local radio stations.
Ports and Airports	Belfast is one of the UK's major ports. The International airport is about 20 miles from Belfast, but there is also a small single-runway airport within the city.	
Electricity	240 volts, as in the rest of the UK	
Internet Domain	.uk	
Telephone	The international code is 00 44, as in the UK.	
Time	Greenwich Mean Time, plus 1 hr. in summer	

LAND &
PEOPLE

GEOGRAPHY AND CLIMATE

Set at the very edge of Europe, battered by the
Atlantic but warmed by the Gulf Stream, Ireland
is tethered a few miles off the coasts of Wales,
England, and Scotland. But in its shape—the
smooth east coast and the straggling indented
west coast—it seems to be reaching out across the
Atlantic Ocean toward America, where so many
of its sons and daughters now live.

Ireland's position and the nature of the land
itself has shaped the way of life of the people and
their attitudes toward themselves and others.

Ireland is famous for its greenness, and this greenness has become part of the Irish national identity: the national flag is green, white, and orange; the sportsmen and women play in green; even the telephone boxes are green.

Connemara on the west coast, which faces the great ocean head on, is not green. It is a brown, rugged, and bleak place of stones and of few trees. Yet it has a great natural grandeur and it is here that the old ways are best preserved. In the northwest is Donegal, distinctively beautiful, with magnificent beaches. Just south of Donegal, Sligo was immortalized by the poems of W. B. Yeats.

The Donegal Highlands in the northeast rise to about 700 feet (about 230 meters), but even Slieve Donard, the highest peak of the Mountains of Mourne, sweeps down to the sea from a height of just 2,786 feet (849 meters). The Wicklow Mountains in the east rise to a similar height. In the south the wonderfully named Macgillycuddy's

Pembroke Branch Tel. 6689575

Reeks are a little higher, making them the highest mountains in the whole island.

Ireland is a country of hills and plains, but above all it is a land of rivers and lakes; the Republic alone has 537 square miles (1,390 square kilometers) of water. Most people have heard of the beautiful Lakes of Killarney, but few realize Lough Neagh in Ulster is the largest lake in the British Isles. All this water is put to good use: hydroelectricity generates about 6 percent of Ireland's electrical needs.

The "pleasant waters of the river Lee," the Blackwater, the Suir, the Nore, the Barrow, the Liffey, from whose water Guinness is supposed to be made, the Boyne where a famous battle was fought, and the Lagan on which the city of Belfast stands, all flow toward the east. Only the Bann flows north; and the Shannon, two hundred fifty miles long and the longest river in the British Isles, flows south.

To the north of the Shannon lies the lovely county of Clare, with the unique landscape of the rocky Burren country.

Galway, in its famous bay, is the major city of the west and looks to the sea rather than the land.

No rivers flow into the sea in Connaught, but there is no shortage of water. The west is often seen as the most distinctively Irish part of the country—it is certainly the wettest. The water-bearing clouds fresh from the Atlantic strike the rising ground and the rain comes down in bucketfuls. But there's still plenty left for the rest of the country.

For in truth the "Emerald" Isle's color derives from its climate, which involves a certain amount of rain. Even the driest parts around Dublin get 150 days of rain a year, and an annual total of 29.5 inches (75 cm) of rainfall. Bring your umbrellas and waterproof gear even in the sunniest months of May and June, but be prepared equally for beautiful sunny days in February or November. The skies are often overcast, but the sun is always ready to surprise you by showing her face when she is least expected—the sun is a female noun in Irish, and was once a goddess. The combination of sunshine and moisture makes for wonderful sunsets over Galway Bay and for glorious rainbows. And all you have to do is find the foot of a rainbow to claim a Leprechaun's crock of gold.

If an Irishman tells you it's "a grand soft day" he means it is raining gently but the day is quite pleasantly warm. For the climate is surprisingly mild, milder than might be expected in northern latitudes thanks to the warm Gulf Stream that washes Ireland's shores. The rain rarely turns to snow, and temperatures in the east range from about 39°F (4°C) in January to 68°F (20°C) in August.

The mild damp climate affects many aspects of Irish culture. The ancient Irish clans roamed widely to rustle each other's cattle, and epic poems like *The Cattle Raid of Cooley* were recited about their deeds. These heroes never settled down to become respectable farmers tilling fields of wheat because wheat does not grow well in this climate. The rainfall is wonderful for grass, but wheat tends to rot. Even today 90 percent of Irish agricultural land is down to pasture or rough grazing.

About a third of Ireland is made up of a central plain covered with clay, deposited when the ice sheets withdrew at the end of the last ice age, which retains a lot of surface water from the copious rainfall. Here peat moss thrives and over thousands of years has built up into peat bogs, a sort of embryonic coal—though the island has very little true coal. Most of the bogs have been drained so the peat can be cut for fuel. The scent of a peat fire (the Irish often call peat "turf") drifting from a cottage chimney is unforgettable.

Ireland is known for the excellence of its beef and dairy products and Ireland is the biggest beef exporter in Europe. The green pastures of the central plain are devoted mainly to dairying, but also raise fine pigs, and the wonderful grass of the Curragh breeds famous horses. Beef cattle from the west are sent eastward to the richer pastures of

Meath for fattening. James Joyce writes in *Ulysses* of a sturdy young woman being "beef to the heels" like a Mullingar heifer. There are few golden fields of corn; instead oats and potatoes are grown, and in the comparatively dry and sunny southeast, barley—Cork is famous for its brewing and distilling.

West of the west coast are the Aran Islands. These rocky places, battered by the seas and gales of the Atlantic, have an emotional significance to Irish people out of all proportion to the number of their inhabitants.

People have lived here for 4,000 years, and the islands are a treasure house of antiquities and Celtic remains. Gaelic is still many people's first language, though English is today heard almost as often. Here the old traditions and folklore lasted longer than on the mainland. The way of life was hard. Seaweed and sand were carried from the shore to cover the barren rocks with some sort of soil, which had to be held in by stone walls to keep it from being blown back into the sea. The tiny fields supported at best a single cow or a few scraggy sheep. To catch fish the islanders would brave the Atlantic rollers in *currachs*—frail canvas boats that they rowed with remarkable courage and skill.

Nowadays the island economy is rather more prosperous. In the course of the summer season 100,000 visitors arrive, and many of them take away with them one of the famous Aran sweaters (or *ganseys*) knitted in complex and individual Celtic designs.

Don't Overdo It!

Many visitors like to stock up on distinctive Irish clothing—Aran sweaters, tweeds, and the like. By all means wear them while in the country but be careful not to overdo it; a visitor who wears a lot of traditional clothing might be the subject of a certain sly humor.

Northern Ireland, which comprises only about a sixth of the island, contains nearly a quarter of its population; most live in the east near Belfast, though it is easy to escape into areas of real peace.

The North's physical geography differs little from the rest of Ireland. You will sometimes hear the North called "Ulster," though this is not strictly correct—the old kingdom of Ulster also included three counties now in the Republic.

The weather is no less rainy than that of the Republic, and the winters are equally mild.

Old Ulsterman: *If you can see Carickfergus Castle on the opposite side of Belfast Lough that means its going to rain.*
Visitor: *And if you can't see it?*
Old Ulsterman: *That means it's already raining.*

The damp climate and pure water were well suited to the cultivation and preparation of flax, and Northern Ireland was world famous for its linen.

Finally, Ireland is the best place to be on the planet if you want to avoid earthquakes. No epicenter has ever been found anywhere on the entire island!

IRISH SOCIETY AND PEOPLE
The pattern of life in Ireland has come to resemble that of its neighbors. Superficially, it can be hard to tell an English, Scots, or Welsh person from someone from Ireland. People dress the same, speak the same language, have many of the same tastes.

This was not always so and underneath the surface there are significant differences—many born of historical experience. To understand the Irish you must be aware of the events that have shaped and still shape their thoughts and feelings. Ireland is a complex place where the apparent similarity to other Western countries can be misleading. A little trouble taken to learn its customs, etiquette, and traditions will be amply rewarded.

The English are famously ignorant of Irish history—if they had understood it a bit better things might have been different. On the other hand, the Irish are steeped in their history, both real and mythical. Their history and their religion have forged the national consciousness—which is why, throughout this book, you will find plenty of snippets of history.

For nearly eight hundred years England ruled Ireland. During much of that time effective English government could only be imposed within fifty miles of Dublin, the so-called Pale of Dublin—those outside English control being considered barbarians and so "beyond the Pale." But at other times English rule extended throughout the island and was often harsh, repressive, and bitterly resented.

An Open Society

If yesterday the English were the ruling class and the Irish were the ruled, today the most obvious characteristic of Irish society is its openness and lack of any obvious class structure. Everybody uses first names except, significantly, priests and nuns, who are always Father this or Sister that. The Anglo-Irish, once the landowning gentry, still exist, but are tolerated rather than revered— especially since Irish farmers are no longer tenants but own their land.

Ireland scarcely experienced the eighteenth and nineteenth century industrialization that created the working-class/middle-class division in English society, except to some extent in what is now Northern Ireland, and there the fiercely egalitarian nature of the dominant Presbyterian Church militated against obvious class differences.

The result is that Irish society is fairly heterogeneous, with most people having similar roots in rural culture. To suggest that there is absolutely no distinctive Irish urban working-class culture is an exaggeration—as witness the plays of Sean O'Casey and, more recently, the novels of Roddy Doyle. Another famous writer,

Brendan Behan, was proud of being the working-class son of a Dublin painter and decorator. Yet his mother's family came from a family of farmers in County Meath, while his mother's brother, the poet Paedar Kearney, actually wrote the Irish national anthem, "The Soldiers' Song."

Nevertheless, given Dublin's size, a rural/urban divide is inevitable. Dublin in the new millennium is awash with new money as successful entrepreneurs and entertainers pay lavish sums for the houses of the old English rulers. "Dublin 4" actually refers to a postal area, but the term is used to sum up the cosmopolitan attitudes of the urban elite who live there (as opposed to the old sturdy rural values of "the plain people of Ireland"!). Then there are the so-called "chattering classes"—intellectuals, politicians, bureaucrats, and professionals found in certain southside Dublin pubs. There is even a lively interest in genealogical matters, and not just from expatriate families. Although Eire does not grant aristocratic titles it does have a Chief Herald whose office grants coats of arms, and there are several organizations that can help you trace your Irish roots. Country-dwellers can feel out of touch with city people, and tend to distrust them, though less so as change percolates into the countryside.

About one-tenth of the labor force is involved in farming—much higher than the European Union average but a long way removed from the idealistic view of Ireland expressed by President Eamon de Valera in his 1943 St. Patrick's Day broadcast:

A land whose countryside would be bright
with cosy homesteads, whose fields and villages
would be . . . joyous with the romping of sturdy
children, the contests of athletic youths and the
laughter of comely maidens . . . .

Status

By and large those people perceived to be at the
top of Irish society come from the new class of
entrepreneurs, some of whom are extremely
wealthy by any international yardstick. Status is
generally derived either from wealth or talent.
What people achieve is determined by their own
efforts rather than by background and education.

The Irish revere their dead heroes, but toward
the living they are likely to feel less reverential.
Irish culture is naturally artistic, particularly in
the arts of poetry, music, and drama, but those
who excel in these fields are seen as part of
society, not some sort of elite.

Irish Irreverence

In England the eminent poet Seamus Heaney
(who died in 2013) accepted the post of Professor
of Poetry at Oxford University, and was offered
the title of Poet Laureate, which as a republican he
refused. In Ireland he was respected and admired
but not revered or put on a pedestal. Indeed
he was sometimes gently mocked as "Famous
Seamus."

Tax Free Art

Artists, especially writers, are attracted to Ireland by a taxation system that allows the first 50,000 euros of income from artistic activity to be tax free. The presence of so many artists from around the world has been a major influence on society over the last quarter-century.

THE IMPORTANCE OF HISTORY TO THE IRISH

There is probably no country in the world where the attitudes and values of its modern inhabitants are so much the product of their history. Certain key events or concepts have become part of the Irish mind-set. You will hear people speaking of the "Island of Saints and Scholars," or perhaps refer to the "Flight of the Earls," "the Plantation of Ulster," the "Curse of Cromwell," "the Penal Laws," "the Protestant Ascendancy," "the 98," Robert Emmet's speech from the dock, or "The Liberator O'Connell." Northern Protestants will talk about "the Apprentice Boys of Derry" and "King Billy and the Battle of the Boyne." And all spoken of as if they were still living issues—as to many Irish people they are!

Land of Saints and Scholars

Ireland has been inhabited since about 7,000–8,000 BCE when the first colonists arrived from Scotland, probably then linked to Ireland by land. Some 4,000 years later the Neolithic, or Stone

Age, inhabitants arrived by boat from Britain and constructed massive religious monuments such as the megalithic tomb at New-Grange (within easy driving distance of Dublin and well worth a visit).

The sixth century BCE brought the Celts, and a dynamic era of arts and crafts: Ireland rejoices in the largest collection of prehistoric gold artifacts found in Western Europe; you can see them at the National Museum in Dublin.

Every Irishman knows that what sets Ireland apart from most of Europe is the fact that it was never part of the Roman Empire, at a time when most of Europe had submitted to the Roman yoke. In fact the Romans were not interested in occupying a country that had few metals of its own, and could not grow the grain needed to feed their armies.

Greco-Roman classical learning and literacy came to Ireland with the introduction of Christianity and writing in the fifth century. Latin civilization fused with the Celtic decorative tradition to produce such masterpieces as the Ardagh Chalice, the Book of Durrow, and the Book of Kells.

Sometimes the monks grew bored with the slow, painstaking copying of the Gospels, and scribbled short lyrics in the margins of their work, like this, written in an eighth-century copy of St. Paul's Epistles.

I and Pangur Ban, my cat,
'Tis a like task we are at;
Hunting mice is his delight,
Hunting words I sit all night . . .

Better far than praise of men
'Tis to sit with book and pen . . .
(Extract from *Pangur Ban*, trans. Robin Flower)

Among the hundreds of monasteries founded at this time were the great centers of Clonmacnoise in County Offaly, and Monastarboice in County Louth. This was a golden age for Ireland, which became a refuge for classical scholarship and Christian learning in a Europe that was elsewhere sinking back into barbarity. Hence the pride in being the "Island of Saints and Scholars"!

The Vikings and St. Brendan

The Viking invasions from the ninth century onward brought death and destruction but also trade, currency, and the foundation of most of the major towns including Dublin. It was in the ninth century that *The Voyage of St. Brendan* was

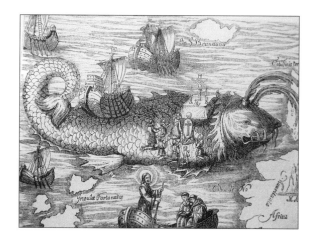

written, which seems to describe a journey across
the Atlantic to America by the Irish saint.

Tara and the High Kings

All this time Ireland was divided into separate
kingdoms. There were "High Kings" (*Ard-Ri* in
Gaelic) based at the hill of Tara in County Meath,
with a great hall 700 feet (240 meters) long, but
their title was honorary and sacred, and they
wielded no real power over other rulers. Yet
these various kingdoms shared a language, a set
of laws, the Brehon Laws, and a common artistic,
literary, and musical culture. As early as the third
century CE the High King, Cormac, founded
what was in effect a royal academy to promote
poetry and the law.

In 1014 the High King Brian Boru defeated
the Norsemen at the Battle of Clontarf—typically

he was also fighting other Irishmen, the men of Leinster having sided with the Vikings!

The Normans

An Anglo-Norman adventurer, the Earl of Pembroke, known as Strongbow, arrived in 1170, invited across by an Irish king who was quarreling with the High King. The mounted and mailed Norman knights with their big horses, lances, archers (the Irish only had slings), and impregnable castles were in a different class from the *kernes*, the Irish foot soldiers. They soon controlled all of Ireland except for part of Ulster, and for the first time Ireland was theoretically part of the kingdom of England.

Very little of the island actually came under direct English rule. Most of the local Norman and native Irish chiefs were a law unto themselves, and the King of England's writ did not run beyond the Pale, some fifty miles round Dublin.

More Irish than the Irish!

The Norman barons intermarried with the Irish, adopted Irish ways and laws, and even learned to speak Gaelic, so that Norman surnames like Fitzgerald, Costello, or Butler, now seem as Irish as O'Connor or O'Brian. Indeed the Norman lords were accused of being *Hibernicis ipsis Hibernior—* "More Irish than the Irish." Be warned: the visitor who tries too zealously to copy Irish ways is often today ridiculed as "More Irish than the Irish."

The Flight of the Earls and the Plantation of Ulster

Only in the late Tudor era and the sixteenth century was Ireland beyond the Pale brought anything like under control. This century also saw the start of the great religious divide between Protestants and Catholics, since the introduction of the Elizabethan prayer book was the first serious attempt to impose the Protestant Reformation on the Irish people. In Tudor times Ulster in the North was the heartland of the native Irish. Its great chieftain, Hugh O'Neill, Earl of Tyrone, was brought up in Queen Elizabeth's court. Yet when England was at war with Spain he and his powerful neighbor, Hugh O'Donnell, marched their men all the way to the south to try to rescue a Spanish force besieged in Kinsale. They were routed.

O'Neill was pardoned in 1603, but hated to serve where he had formerly ruled. In 1607 he and the Earl of Tyrconnell, Hugh O'Donnell's son, fled to France and then Rome. The "Flight of the Earls" was followed by the dispossession of many Catholics in Ulster, and their lands were given to Englishmen and, especially, Scots—the two realms having just been united under James I of England (and VI of Scotland). These colonists would be hated by the Irish they displaced and would support the Crown. This was the "Plantation of Ulster," and it explains why so many people in Ulster have Scottish names, are Presbyterians like the Scots, and are still loyal to the British Crown.

The Curse of Cromwell

In 1641, just before the English Civil War, the Irish rebelled and the question of who should control the forces sent against them actually precipitated the war. During the war they theoretically sided with the King, Charles I, and after the King was defeated and executed they were savagely suppressed by the leader of the Parliamentary army in Ireland: Oliver Cromwell. The massacres following the sieges of Drogheda and Wexford in 1649 and his seizure of great swathes of his Irish opponents' lands have made Cromwell a name loathed in the South: to put the "Curse of Cromwell" on someone is a terrible imprecation. By contrast Belfast has a major thoroughfare named after him! Cromwell settled many of his troops in Ireland but they became assimilated like so many before them.

King Billy, the Apprentice Boys, and the Battle of the Boyne

When the exiled Charles II returned to England to accept the throne in 1660 many Irishmen hoped to get their lands back. But Charles was only restored at the invitation of Parliament and could do nothing. In 1685 Charles's brother James, a Catholic, became King. James II made himself so unpopular that William of Orange, the Protestant Dutch ruler (married to James's sister Mary), was invited to take over the English throne.

James turned to Ireland, where in 1689 he attempted to stage a comeback and was welcomed by the Catholic population. They had backed the wrong horse. James was denied entry to the City of Londonderry when thirteen Protestant apprentice boys seized the keys and shut the gates in his face. Thirty thousand Protestants were besieged in the city for 105 days, while an English fleet looked on and failed to help them. To this day Protestant Loyalists still prefer to trust to themselves rather than the English.

When called on to give in they replied "No Surrender," and this phrase has been the watchword of the Northern Irish Protestants ever since.

On July 12, 1690, William of Orange, riding a white horse, defeated the Catholic Irish under James at the Battle of the Boyne. King Billy and his white horse are still to be seen painted on the side of many Belfast end-of-terrace houses, together with the words "1690 No Surrender!"

James fled to Dublin, where he complained that the Irish (who actually fought very hard) had run away. A lady present remarked "Your Majesty won the race!" James II is not a popular figure in Irish history and it would be as well not to translate his nickname, *Seamus a Chaca*. It is not unconnected with what flows through sewers!

The Penal Laws

The Protestant victory led to the enactment of the "Penal Laws" against Catholics in 1695. These placed severe restrictions on landownership by Catholics, which caused many landowners to convert to the Anglican Church of Ireland. By 1778 when the penal laws began to be repealed only 5 percent of the land was Catholic owned.

The Protestant Ascendancy

The eighteenth century was the age of the "Protestant Ascendancy" when many of Ireland's great houses were built and Dublin acquired its beautiful redbrick Georgian squares. Dublin became a fashionable center, and Ireland had its own Parliament (Catholics were excluded of course). The old Parliament building is now the Bank of Ireland.

It was said that "the Church of Ireland fell asleep during the eighteenth century," but if the Anglican clergy of Ireland were not distinguished for their piety, several became famous in other ways. Jonathan Swift, author of *Gulliver's Travels* and other satirical works, was Dean of St. Patrick's Cathedral, Bishop Berkeley was a famous philosopher, and

John Hervey wrote an important account of the court of George II. Nonclerical products of the Protestant Ascendancy include the chemist Robert Boyle, the politician Edward Burke, and the writers Richard Sheridan and Oliver Goldsmith.

The United Irishmen and the '98

In the late eighteenth century the American and French Revolutions inspired uprisings by the mainly Protestant "United Irishmen" led by Wolfe Tone and Lord Edward Fitzgerald. In 1796 a French fleet of thirty-five ships crammed with thousands of troops fresh from victories all over Europe anchored off Bantry Bay. But a week of fierce gales made it impossible for them to land and they sailed away.

The English soldiers' cruel floggings of anyone they thought might reveal information about the United Irishmen were largely responsible for the rising known as "the '98" two years later. Now no well-armed French professionals arrived to take on the British. Instead the Irish had to make do with their traditional weapons—homemade pikes manufactured by the local blacksmiths. After some minor successes the rebels were easily crushed at the battle of Vinegar Hill outside Wexford. In the North the Presbyterians, who also suffered under the Penal Laws, actively supported the rebellion, and Henry Joy McCracken led a force that captured Antrim town from the British garrison.

The failed rebellion led to the incorporation of Ireland into the United Kingdom by the Act of Union of 1801, and the end of the Irish Parliament.

Robert Emmet led an abortive rising in Dublin in 1803, which proved a fiasco, but his speech from the dock when he was condemned to death has rung down the years.

Let no man write my epitaph. When my country takes her place among the nations of the earth, then and not till then let my epitaph be written.

The Liberator

Daniel O'Connell, born into one of the few remaining families of prosperous Catholic landowners, is still known as "the Liberator." He held mass meetings—one at Tara numbered nearly a million people— and pressured the British government into granting basic civil rights and full Catholic emancipation in 1829. Irish Catholics could now sit in Parliament at Westminster, Catholic bishops and archbishops were accepted, and many Catholic churches were built.

THE MAKING OF MODERN IRELAND
The Great Famine and Emigration

A series of events since 1845 have had a colossal significance in defining not just the political and economic structure of modern Ireland but also its culture. These key events are the Famine and

Emigration, Evictions and the Land Acts, the
Gaelic Revival, the Easter Rising and the "Tan
War," the Treaty of 1921, and the Irish Civil War.

Although Ireland is so much farther from
America than it is from Britain, separated by
the "wild and wasteful" Atlantic, since the mid-
nineteenth century there has been a great sense of
kinship between the Americans and the Irish. When
John F. Kennedy was elected President, many Irish
people saw him as "their" president. Galway even
renamed its main square "Kennedy Square."

The key occurrence in this orientation toward
America was the Great Hunger of the 1840s. Folk
memories of those terrible times are an important
facet of the Irish psyche.

The population of Ireland had burgeoned in
the early nineteenth century. The country people
became dependent on a single crop, the potato,
which was nutritious and easy to grow. But when
the entire crop was destroyed by blight in the mid-

1840s a million died and huge numbers of others emigrated to America.

Three years in a row the potato crop failed, and the suffering of the people became dreadful. And all the while the British government did virtually nothing about it.

There were widespread deaths from starvation and from typhus, known as "famine fever." Even those who fled to America often died in the crowded, unsanitary "coffin ships." And all the while, in accordance with the new belief in Free Trade, food was being exported in bulk to Britain. All this led to a terrible sense of betrayal.

> *I ventured through the parish this day to ascertain the condition of the inhabitants and although a man not easily moved, I confess myself unmanned by the extent and density of suffering I witnessed, more especially among the women and little children, crowds of whom were seen scattered over the turnip fields, like a flock of famished crows devouring the raw turnips, and mostly half naked, shivering in the snow and sleet, uttering exclamations of despair, while their children were screaming with hunger. I am a match for anything else I may meet here, but this I cannot stand.*
> (Captain Wynne, Inspecting Officer, West Clare, 1846)

The "Great Hunger" sowed in Irish hearts a profound bitterness not toward the English people but toward the English government. It is the central defining event of Ireland's history.

By contrast huge gratitude was felt toward the people and government of the United States for taking in so many of its victims. Both these feelings remain a very significant factor in Irish life even today.

What captivity was to the Jews, exile has been to the Irish. America and American influence has educated them.
(Oscar Wilde, 1889)

It was many years before the Irish population got back to half what it had been in 1840. At least a million died, but the rest of the population loss was caused by the huge scale of emigration to America, Australia, New Zealand, and Canada. Indeed there are still said to be more Irish living in New York than in Dublin. Thousands of men came to mainland Britain, leaving behind their families and womenfolk, to labor on the new railways as "navvies"— short for navigators. "The Great Hunger" partly explains the much-admired lack of crowding in Ireland, the spaciousness, the quiet roads

The Irish Have Long Memories
The Great Famine of one hundred and sixty and more years ago is not forgotten. In 2015 there was an Irish TV series about it and even a feature film detailing the role Turkey had played in famine relief, while in 1994 Sinead O'Connor had a hit with a song simply entitled "Famine."

Soon after the Famine a new word entered the vocabulary of Rebellion: "Fenian." Named after the *Fianna*, the legendary Finn McCool's band of heroes, the Fenians were pledged to wage guerrilla war against the British, and American-Irish emigrants held rallies to raise money for them.

The world's first submarine was invented clandestinely by John Philip Holland (1841–1914), a former member of the Catholic teaching order, the Christian Brothers. It was known as "the Fenian Ram" and was financed by the American Irish in the hope that it would prove the answer to Britain's naval supremacy.

But the Irish cause was to make its greatest gains in this period by political, rather than by violent action.

The Home Rule Movement
Toward the end of the nineteenth century Charles Stewart Parnell, leader of the Irish Parliamentary Party in the British House of Commons, dominated Irish politics. His aim was to achieve "Home Rule," with Ireland remaining subject to Queen Victoria but governing itself. His eighty MPs were in a powerful position since they held the balance between the two main parties, the Conservatives and Liberals, but he was assisted by the fact that Gladstone, the Liberal leader, sympathized with his views.

Parnell fought savagely against absentee Irish landlords living in England who were evicting their small tenants to consolidate their Irish lands into more viable and profitable units. It was Parnell who suggested in a speech in 1880 that those responsible for carrying out the actual evictions should be ostracized. "You must show what you think of him . . . by isolating him from the rest of his kind as if he were a leper of old, you must show him your detestation of the crime he has committed."

Boycotting

In so doing Parnell introduced a new word into the English language. The first victim of this treatment was a Captain Boycott, who was a land agent in County Mayo. Ever since the word "boycott" has been used for this sort of action.

Parnell fell from office because it became known he was having an affair with a married woman, which alienated him from his Catholic following. He was deposed in December 1890 and was dead within the year.

Gladstone proposed several Home Rule bills that were defeated in the House of Lords, but he and his party had more success with laws that enabled tenants to buy their own land. The state bought out the landlords and advanced mortgages to the former tenants that worked out to be a lot less than they had been paying as rent. Further "Land Purchase Acts" in 1903 and 1909 led to the principle of compulsory sale by the landlords, so that even before Independence the Catholic former tenants already owned the greater part of the agricultural land in Ireland.

The Irish Love of the Land
The Land laws explain why Irish agriculture takes the form of thousands of small farms, rather than large tracts as in America or even Britain. Today the average holding is still only 32 hectares. Irish farmers are fiercely attached to their land, which for so many years was taken from them.

Independence and Partition
Partly because of the Land Acts, political action took something of a back seat for a while (apart from Trade Union agitation in Dublin led by Liverpool Irishman James Larkin). Instead there was the Gaelic Revival: a reassertion of Irish culture that had immense influence in reviving Irish self-respect and awareness of a unique national identity.

When the First World War broke out in 1914 thousands of Irishmen volunteered for the British Army. So when to everyone's surprise a rising occurred in Dublin at Easter

1916 and the insurgents seized the General Post Office, the rebels were far from popular. But the brutal execution of the leaders (two who escaped execution were a Corkman, Michael Collins, and a Spaniard with an Irish mother, Eamon de Valera) revived all the old anti-British feelings. The poet W. B. Yeats, one of the leaders of the Celtic Revival, wrote that all was:

> . . . *changed, changed utterly:*
> *A terrible beauty is born.*

A minor political party called *Sinn Fein* (pronounced "SHIN-fain" and meaning "Ourselves Alone") became identified with the rising, and its members captured most of the Irish seats in the 1918 Parliament following the First World War.

Shortly afterward, guerrilla war broke out in Ireland. The Irish Republican Army under the legendary leadership of Michael Collins fought against the British Auxiliary Forces, ex-servicemen known as the "Black and Tans" from the color of their rather makeshift uniforms. Many acts of brutality occurred in the "Tan War" and the British Auxiliary Forces sometimes behaved more like terrorists than disciplined troops.

This struggle, together with the tremendous influence of American public opinion, led to the Anglo–Irish Treaty in 1921, whereby twenty-six of the thirty-two counties were granted the status of a "Free State," but remained subservient to London in various important matters. The refusal of many

Irishmen to accept these limitations led to the
Civil War of 1921–2.

The Origin of the Main Irish Political Parties
The party that refused to accept the treaty became
known as *Fianna Fail* (pronounced "Fina-fall").
Those who were prepared to accept it ultimately
became the *Fine Gael* (pronounced "Feen-
gale"). They won the war but at the cost of the
assassination of Michael Collins. Fianna Fail and
Fine Gael became the two main political parties in
the Irish Parliament, divided not by their differing
policies but by their memories.

The 1921 Treaty highlighted the problem of
Northern Ireland. Before the First World War the
northern Protestants led by the famous lawyer
Sir Edward Carson had categorically rejected
Home Rule. Rather than live in a country
controlled by the Catholic majority they declared

that "Ulster would fight and Ulster would be right!" and raised an army of 40,000 men armed with smuggled German rifles to show they meant business.

The Orange Order and the Twelfth of July

Every July 12 you will see men parading through the cities of Northern Ireland on the anniversary of the Battle of the Boyne. They wear orange sashes, bowler hats, and white gloves, and sometimes break into a curious shuffling dance step known as the "Orange Shuffle." They are accompanied by bands—silver bands and brass bands, but especially fife and drum bands. They are members of "the Orange Order," a society founded in 1795 dedicated to defending the Protestant religion. At one time it was almost banned, but from the mid-nineteenth century it burgeoned and has taken the lead in opposing the idea of a united independent Ireland.

With the outbreak of the First World War the Ulster Volunteers patriotically enlisted in the British Army but their German rifles were hidden away in case they should be needed later. It was partly because of this threat, but more in gratitude for the "blood sacrifice" of these volunteers (who were killed almost to a man in the Battle of the Somme) that six of the nine counties of Ulster were separated from the rest of Ireland to remain part of the United Kingdom. We are still living with the results of this division nearly a hundred years later.

Southern Ireland, or Eire, became a republic in all but name after Fianna Fail, led by Eamon De Valera, came to power in 1932, and especially after his new constitution of 1937. Eire was actually neutral in the Second World War, but it was not until 1948 that the "Free State" declared itself a republic and left the British Commonwealth.

Throughout the early years of independence the Irish government maintained a highly protectionist economy, and Ireland had a predictably insular psychology. It remained a largely rural backwater: peaceful, charming, but with a markedly lower standard of living than its neighbors and an economy still dominated by the British market.

To add to Ireland's difficulties, De Valera refused to continue repaying the British government loans that had enabled farmers to buy their land. The result was an economic war that lasted six years and did nothing to improve the Irish economy or North/South relations, except perhaps between the thousands of smugglers on both sides of the border.

De Valera's new constitution of 1937 outlawed both contraception and divorce and implied, nicely but categorically, that a woman's place was in the home. Whereas elsewhere in Europe the number of women in work was constantly increasing, in Ireland the figure decreased. Emigration was still the easiest way for the young and energetic to improve their lot—and it is claimed that of the generation of men born between 1931 and 1941, 80 percent emigrated.

America and Australia remained the preferred destinations, but the chances of returning were small. Like the navvies before them many young Irishmen left the countryside to earn better money in England in the building trade. Most of them intended to make enough money to return to Ireland and marry, but all too many never did.

All this has changed drastically in the last sixty years. Ireland today is hugely different from what it was in the 1950s. And the transformation is continuing at breakneck speed.

THE MAIN CITIES

Irish cities are usually compact, so that you are aware that they are set in the countryside. Belfast is a typical industrial conurbation but you have only to look upward to see the empty hills that surround three sides of the city. Even in Dublin, much the largest of Irish cities, you can catch glimpses of the blue hills and a short drive brings you into unspoiled country.

Dublin

Dublin is both the Irish capital and the capital of the province of Leinster. Like most of Ireland's great cities it was founded by the Vikings (called "Danes" in Ireland). *Dubh-linn* literally means "Blackpool," but that wasn't poetic enough for the founders of the Irish State. Its official Irish name is *Baile Atha Cliath* ("BOLL-yah AW-hah CLEE-ah"), "the Town on the Ford of the Hurdles," commemorating Conor McNessa, King of Ulster, who built a bridge of hurdles across the swollen River Liffey. But everyone calls it Dublin.

It is home to well over a million today, more if you count the outlying suburbs. Dublin exports,

among other things, stout and whiskey, glass and pharmaceuticals. It also makes microprocessors and is the seat of Parliament.

Despite unforgivable municipal vandalism in the 1960s and 1970s, Dublin is still, at least in part, a town of lovely Georgian squares and of open spaces. Phoenix Park is the largest walled park in Europe, and herds of deer roam in it.

Naturally Dublin has the National Museum and National Art Gallery, but Ireland's greatest

national treasure, the eighth-century Book of Kells, said to be the most beautiful book in the world, is to be found in Trinity College. Trinity was founded in 1591 to promote Anglicanism and is now known as Dublin University. University College, for Catholics, where James Joyce studied, became part of the, separate, National University of Ireland in 1909. There is also now a third university in the city: the Dublin City University.

There are far too many interesting sights to list here. Dublin even has two cathedrals, both Anglican—the Catholics have to make do with a "pro-Cathedral" in a back street. Serious tourists can buy one of the many good city guides.

Cork

Cork (population 190,000) is the Republic's second city. It is reputedly the friendliest city in Ireland and its citizens the most talkative in a generally garrulous country. They were also famous rebels. The Cork Column was one of the most successful units in the war against the Black and Tans, and in retaliation in 1920 they deliberately set Cork on fire and killed its Sinn Fein Lord Mayor. His successor, Terence MacSwiney, died in jail in London after a hunger strike.

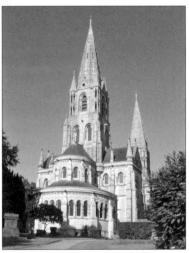

Cork City is on the River Lee; its streets are built over waterways where ships would have been anchored. Like Dublin it was founded by the Danes. But before that St. Finbar had established a monastery there. St. Finn Barre's Anglican Cathedral is a splendid Gothic Revival building built between 1865 and 1880.

Cork is well known for its gin, its whiskey, for Beamish stout, and for Father Matthew. When Cork people talk of "the Statue," they mean that of Father Theobald Matthew (his name is spelled "Mathew" on its plinth). Father Matthew founded the Catholic temperance movement that became the Pioneers. The success of the Pioneers is one of several reasons

why the image of the drunken Irish is far from true of most Irishmen, especially people in the countryside.

The city's port, called Cobh, has Ireland's only dedicated cruise terminal—in the past it was the departure point for millions of Irish people emigrating to North America.

Blarney Castle is in the vicinity, where thousands of tourists lean backward and nearly break their necks in order to kiss an unhygienic bit of rock called the blarney stone in the belief that it will give them the gift of the gab.

Galway

Galway, way out in the west, is the capital of bleakly beautiful Connaught. It is a wonderfully lively city with huge numbers of young people, mainly students, who make up 20 percent of its 72,000 population. It is full of musical pubs, is a center for the Gaelic language, and is the gateway to the Aran Islands.

Limerick
Limerick, on the Shannon estuary, has a rapidly growing population of over 100,000. Founded in 812 it was the capital of the King of Thomond, Brian Boru, who became the High King at Tara and defeated the Vikings at the battle of Clontarf in 1014.

Belfast
Belfast's population is about 280,000, but half a million people live within ten miles of the city, accounting for about a third of the entire population of the province of Northern Ireland. Queen's University was founded in 1845, and the Northern Irish Assembly is at Stormont, a Belfast suburb.

The city was founded in 1177 but remained tiny until the textile industry was stimulated by the

arrival of French Protestants (Huguenots), fleeing persecution in the late seventeenth century. Its location on the deep waters of Belfast Lough made it a great center for shipbuilding—the *Titanic* was built at Harland and Woolff's yard here. The shipbuilding and the linen boom of the nineteenth century meant the population swelled from 20,000 in 1800 to 387,000 in 1911.

The city center has been redeveloped over the last thirty years, and today Belfast has an air of real vitality, helped by the fact the last thirty years have seen a major literary renaissance in Northern Ireland.

By 1939 Belfast had more people than Dublin. But the traditional industries were already in decline, and terrible air raids during the war, together with the effects of the Troubles from 1969 onward, led to a drop in population and high unemployment, which peaked in the 1980s. Quieter times since the cease-fire and the power-sharing agreements of the 1990s seem to be leading to a significant recovery.

Londonderry

Londonderry, or Derry to its mainly Catholic population, is the province's only other major city. It used to be famous for shirt making, but now its industry is largely technology-based—boosted by sizable government grants and American investment. Set on the Foyle estuary in the west of the province it has a population of about 110,000. St. Columba founded the first monastery here

in the sixth century when it was called Derry. It became Londonderry during the plantation of Ulster, when it was handed over to the Corporation of the City of London to be "planted" with English Protestant settlers, though even today two-thirds of its inhabitants are Catholic.

In 1689 the city held out for 105 days against James II's forces before being relieved. The Catholic Bogside area was frequently in the news during the Troubles between 1968 and the 1990s.

POLITICS IN THE REPUBLIC

Eire is a parliamentary democracy with a written constitution and a two-chamber parliament, the *Oireachtas* (pronounced "ERR-ockh-tuss"). The senate, *Seanad Eireann* ("SHAN-ud-AIR-un") has a total of sixty members, forty-nine elected by the Universities and eleven nominated by the Prime Minister, the *Taoiseach* ("TEE-shock").

The important chamber, though, is the house of representatives, the *Dail Eireann*, ("DAW-il AIR-un"), whose 166 members are elected by a complex form of proportional representation.

Elections are every five years. Fundamental changes have to be approved by referendum: divorce (accepted 1995), abortion (rejected 2002), and same-sex marriage (2015) are recent examples. The President, who is directly elected every seven years, does not exercise an executive role. However, supreme command of the defense forces is vested in the President who also receives and credits ambassadors and carries out ceremonial duties. Real power lies with the *Taoiseach* (formally appointed by the President), who sits in the *Dail* as an elected member.

Criticizing politicians is a popular Irish pastime, but the complexity of the Irish political system with its many nuances is beyond most outsiders.

The Garda

The Republic's police force, the *Garda Siachana* ("Garda shickhana"), usually called "the Garda," is unarmed. The Garda are well integrated into the community, and visitors should not hesitate to call on their services.

Up to the 1980s, the civil war that followed independence in 1921 formed a basic dividing line in the Irish political system, though the oldest political party in Ireland is the Labor Party, dating back to the time of James Larkin, the Trade Union leader. The two dominant parties were Fianna Fail and Fine Gael, in effect representing the two sides in the civil war. At the time of writing, however, De Valera's old party the Fianna Fail appears to be in decline, having been held responsible for the collapse of the Irish economy.

At last the hatreds of the civil war seem to have faded away and, aided by a voting system that works against overall majorities for any one party, coalitions seem to have replaced single-party government. In the 2015 cabinet the *Tanaiste* ("TARN-ash-ta"), or Deputy Prime Minister, was Joan Burton, the leader of the Labor Party, the second largest party. Several new parties have emerged, notably the Green Party, but more strikingly Sinn Fein, the party supporting the demilitarized IRA (which also contests elections in Northern Ireland) made an impressive comeback in the 2011 elections to the *Dail*.

Back in 1990 the election of a liberal woman, Mary Robinson, as President was such a success that another woman, Mary McAleese, succeeded her. This shift away from old stereotypes was also marked by an amendment to articles 2 and 3 of the Irish Constitution, which claimed Northern Ireland as part of a United Ireland. Henceforward union would require the consent of the people of the North. Equally remarkably, in 2011 Queen Elizabeth became the first British monarch to visit the Republic, where she and the President made speeches of reconciliation and friendship.

POLITICS IN NORTHERN IRELAND

For years "The Troubles" in the North plagued all Ireland. They flared up in 1969, and in the following twenty-five years 3,500 people were killed. The issues are complicated yet also simple. Just over half the people are of Scots (mainly) or English stock, "Plantation Protestants" who have no desire to break with Britain and join the Catholic Irish of the Republic. The rest are native Irish Catholics, many of whom would prefer to be part of a united independent Ireland.

And just to muddle things even more, everybody in Ireland, North and South, is entitled to an Irish passport, and all Irish citizens have full rights of citizenship in the United Kingdom!

But, though some violence still occurs occasionally, Northern Ireland has been transformed by the cease-fire of October 1994 and the Good Friday Agreement of 1998, which led to the establishment of the power-sharing Northern Irish Assembly at Stormont. The EU and free trade have also done a lot to break down economic barriers between the two Irelands and may help dissolve other barriers as well. Today Northern Ireland has much to offer the visitor or businessperson.

WHAT IS THE GOOD FRIDAY AGREEMENT?

The Good Friday Agreement of 1998 provided a three-stranded solution. There is an elected Assembly and Executive, representative of both political traditions in Northern Ireland, and there are cross-border bodies to develop cooperation between both parts of the island. An East–West dimension is designed to improve relationships between Ireland and mainland Britain.

The New Assembly

The Assembly has 108 seats elected by a
form of proportional representation, a vastly
fairer elective system than the old system of
"gerrymandering" that guaranteed Protestant
majorities. Ministerial seats are allocated in direct
proportion to the strengths of the various parties.
If it is to work, both sides will have to tear up a lot
of history books.

The Main Parties

There are twelve political parties, of which five
matter: the Loyalists used to be represented by the
Unionist Party, which was the ruling party from
Partition until the original Stormont Parliament
was abolished in 1972, but they have now been
almost completely eclipsed by The Democratic
Unionists, the party the late Reverend Ian Paisley
founded to defend Protestantism. This is currently
the largest party in the Northern Irish Assembly.

Sinn Fein, the second largest, was the former
political wing of the IRA, but under its leader,
Gerry Adams, it has now emerged in its own right
as the main party of the Catholic Republicans.

Power is essentially shared between these
two parties—making it work has meant both
sides having to forget and forgive a lot of painful
memories.

The moderate parties are the Social Democratic
and Labor Party and the Alliance Party, who both
try to bring Catholics and Protestants together.
The SDLP was founded in 1970 by Gerry Fitt, a

Catholic Union leader, and John Hume, a teacher. In 1996 "Saint John" won the Nobel Peace Prize and donated the money to the poor and to victims of violence in the North.

The Good Friday Agreement was the direct result of discussions between Gerry Adams of Sinn Fein and John Hume, who were later joined by David Trimble of the Unionist Party.

Northern Ireland also has 18 seats in the British Parliament at Westminster, but the Sinn Fein members of parliament, including Gerry Adams himself, cannot take up their seats as they refuse to take the oath of loyalty to the Queen.

The Death Rate in Northern Ireland

Although the Troubles in Northern Ireland have taken up so many newspaper headlines over the years, even during the worst times life went on as usual. Throughout the period no tourist was ever killed and Northern Ireland had the lowest death rate in the whole of the United Kingdom!

VALUES &

ATTITUDES

IRISHNESS

Every Englishman seems to have a fixed idea of
the Irish—from Shakespeare in *Henry V* to the
man next to you in the London pub asking you if
you have heard the joke about the two Irishmen.
However what one Englishman wrote about the
Irish four hundred years ago does perhaps still
have a grain of truth in it. Richard Stanyhurst's
"Description of Ireland" forms part of Holinshed's
Chronicles, published in 1577.

> *The people are thus inclined: religious,*
> *frank, amorous, ireful, sufferable of infinite*
> *pains, very vainglorious, many sorcerers,*
> *excellent horsemen, delighted with wars, great*
> *almsgivers, surpassing in hospitality. . . . The*
> *same being virtuously bred up or reformed,*
> *are such mirrors of holiness and austerity*
> *that other nations retain but a shadow in*
> *comparison of them . . . Greedy of praise they*
> *be and fearful of dishonour.*

Certainly the Irish are religious, love horses, and
the country people are wonderfully hospitable, while

the Irish as a whole give more to charity per head than any nation in Europe. To say they delight in wars may be an exaggeration, but famous soldiers of Irish descent in the two world wars include Lord Kitchener, Field Marshal Montgomery, Earl Alexander of Tunis, Field Marshal Alanbrooke, and Lawrence of Arabia (not to mention Peter O'Toole who played him in the film of the same name). The first winner of the Victoria Cross, the highest British military award, was an Irishman, Charles David Lucas.

If the Irish do not seem austere, remember they are capable of going on hunger strike and "suffering infinite pains" to the extent of starving themselves to death for a cause they believe in.

They are often holy, and Ireland is a land of saints, but also one of scholars, writers, poets, and playwrights. The Irish are proud of their ancient culture: poetry, drama, music, singing, and dance are not something special to be separated off as "the Arts," but part of everyday life. They are the means by which the Irish express their distinct identity.

Then there is Irish folklore, with its heroes, larger than life characters such as Finn McCool or Cúchulainn; its heroines, like Deirdre of the Sorrows; and the stories of the Leprechauns and other fairies. People may or may not believe in them, but they are important as part of the national consciousness.

Are the Irish vainglorious? They speak proudly of their status as "a nation once again" and of the centuries-long struggle that won that freedom.

As to whether they are also "ireful," there is maybe a glimmer of truth in the words Shakespeare gives to Captain Macmorris in *Henry V*: "I do not know you so good a man as myself, so Chrish save me, I will cut off your head."

Greedy of Praise?

Oliver St. John Gogarty, one of the great Irish wits (he appears in Joyce's *Ulysses* as Buck Mulligan), once wrote that "You should never praise one Irishman to another," and Irishmen do perhaps have a tendency to criticize each other. When I asked a prosperous Irish businessman I know if he could give me any tips for the chapter on doing business in Ireland his only response was "The Irish! I wouldn't do business with those b—ds!"

Their religion matters to the Irish. Again history provides the key. For years the penal laws proscribed Catholicism, yet 90 percent of those in the southern counties of Ireland remained true to the old faith. More people attend church in Ireland than anywhere else in Europe. And not just Catholics: many Protestants in the North also see their faith as a central reality in their lives and in their identity as a community.

Everyone in Ireland speaks English, but 100,000 or so can also converse reasonably well in the ancient Irish language. As for the others, if many resent the long hours spent studying its complex grammar at school, they would still hate to see it disappear. People like to use a few familiar phrases in everyday conversation— even if it is only to wish you *Slainte* ("SLARN-cha"), good health! On the other hand, you may sometimes see someone with a little gold harp in their lapel; this is the *fainne* ("FARN-nya"), a symbol that they are an Irish speaker.

The Irish are a passionate people and this sometimes makes them narrow-minded or even bigoted in their opinions. Politics in the Republic of Ireland no longer polarizes people as much as it did in the decades following the brief but vicious civil war. As for the North, twenty-five years of murder and bitterness

have inevitably left traumas, but these are
fading fast beneath a deep desire for peace
on both sides.

Don't Get Involved!

Nevertheless try not to get involved in arguments
about the rights and wrongs of Northern Ireland,
but equally do not worry about visiting the
Province. Nowadays life is back to normal. You
will find a beautiful countryside, a progressive
economy, and a people as friendly, obliging, and
welcoming as everywhere else in Ireland.

Mind you, it might take an effort to avoid
becoming involved in political discussions—the
Irish do love a good argument. But then they
love any kind of talk, being a convivial people,
and are genuinely interested in you and what
you have to say.

Even if you have come to Ireland on business
people will want to find out about you and your
family. You can actually cause offense if you try
to cut through these courtesies and get down
to the work at hand too quickly. Like the man
in the pub who suggests you should "hold your
hour and have another," the Irish are no great
respecters of the tyranny of the clock—if the
talk is good why not let it flow for a while? And
before you condemn them for lackadaisicalness,

don't forget they have escaped from the global financial crisis much more effectively than most other European nations.

THE IRISH VIEW OF THE OUTSIDE WORLD

Parallel with Ireland's economic and social changes has been a remarkable change in the Irish view of the outside world. From the late 1920s onward Ireland's chief ministers were drawn from the leaders of the struggle for independence, men like Eamon de Valera and the former IRA officer Sean McBride, traditionalists concerned with preserving the values they had fought for. The decades after independence were marked by a sense of introversion, a desire to concentrate on domestic matters. Those who did not like this attitude were free to leave—and they did, in their millions.

In 1959 the aging de Valera was replaced by Sean Lamass, who was determined to open up the economy and cut back the loss of so many young people to England, Australia, and America. The abandonment of protectionism in the 1960s signalled a new approach. By the mid-1960s emigration had halved and many who had left had chosen to return to a country that now seemed more progressive and full of opportunity.

IRELAND TODAY

Nowadays Irish people holiday abroad in their thousands and even the elderly have learned they have nothing to fear from the outside world. As for the young people, they now see the world as their oyster, with new graduates often spending several years abroad before returning to take jobs at home. Naturally many go to New York or Sydney, but there are substantial pockets of Irish in places as diverse as continental Europe and Japan. And dealing with significant immigration from Europe, from the USA, and from Irish nationals returning from the UK, is proving a challenge for a country where emigration was the fate of so many for so long. As recently as 1970 farming engaged 20 percent of the workforce—now it's fewer than 5 percent. This huge turnaround has had a profound effect on Irish society.

The European Union

The transformation started in 1972, when both the Republic and Northern Ireland (as part of the United Kingdom) joined the European Union. The EU has benefited Ireland economically by investment in industry, by paying for the rapidly improving road network, by modernizing the fishing fleet, and in a thousand other ways. It has made it possible for the Republic to diversify away from agriculture and its claustrophobic one-on-one relationship with Britain and emerge as a modern European state, increasingly confident in its own distinctive identity. Today the United Kingdom only accounts for about a third of Irish exports and imports. On the other hand, the Irish are losing control of their own economic destiny, with foreign-owned companies responsible for half the total turnover and employing almost half the workforce.

More recently Ireland had good reason to be grateful to the EU. Following the economic boom time of the so-called "Celtic Tiger" the Irish economy collapsed. But the EU and IMF, provided a €67.5 billion "bailout" and in July 2011 cut the interest rate from 6 percent to just over 3.5 percent, also doubling the loan time to fifteen years. The Irish economy was saved.

SEX AND MORALITY

The influence of the EU is all-pervasive and has had an impact well beyond economic matters—in European legislation on sexual equality, for instance. But until recently the Catholic Church remained a powerful conservative moral force. The Republic was

the last nation in Europe to legalize divorce—it was narrowly accepted by referendum in 1995. Contraception, too, is still a controversial issue. Contraceptives were banned in Southern Ireland until 1979.

> *The Catholic Church already possesses an efficient contraceptive. It consists in the word, "No!"*
> (Irish Bishop, speaking in the early 1970s)

Only in 1993 did contraceptives become generally available to everyone over seventeen, while homosexuality was still illegal until that same year. And even in 2015, unless the mother's life is in immediate danger, abortion is contrary to the 8th amendment of the Irish constitution. Even in cases where the pregnancy is the result of rape or incest, or where the foetus has a fatal impairment, women can face up to fourteen years in prison for having an abortion. Nevertheless Irish women still frequently have them: they simply go abroad, usually to the UK.

It is easy but perhaps unfair to attribute the Republic's conservatism in sexual matters solely to the influence of the Catholic Church. Long after legislation was introduced in England, Protestant Northern Ireland continued to prosecute homosexuality, and, except in exceptional cases, abortion still remains illegal.

Yet in less than twenty years sexual mores have been revolutionized in the Republic. In the

2011 election David Norris, an openly gay Irish senator who campaigned for the change in the law, was the most popular candidate for President until he decided not to stand. That same year the census found that over 20 percent of all children in the Republic were born outside marriage (the figure for Northern Ireland in 2012 was 43 percent). But while few young people are worried about chastity before marriage, promiscuity is rare and partners tend to stay together. Within marriage, too, the census found, sexual faithfulness remains strong.

CENSORSHIP

Moral censorship used to be a significant aspect of life in the Republic where a huge list of films and books were banned. Ridicule proved a potent enemy and today none are banned. A major breakthrough occurred in 1994 when the film *Priest*, about sex and scandal in the Catholic Church, was shown publicly in Dublin. There had indeed been any number of sexual scandals within the Church. Around that time an elderly priest died in a gay sauna and two younger priests proved to be on hand to give him the last rites! More recently and much more seriously, the revelations of the sexual abuse of children by priests, and, almost worse, the way it was swept under the carpet by Irish bishops has hugely undermined the respect in which the Catholic Church is held.

Mind Your Language!

The Irish love talk but are no lovers of bad language. The casual use of obscenities in conversation that might not raise an eyebrow in England can cause embarrassment and offense. They have a rather charming habit of defusing obscene words by changing one letter—hence the often heard adjective "fecking." James Joyce's *Ulysses*, which was banned in both England and Ireland when it was published in 1922, is famously sexually explicit. But Joyce knew his countrymen well and the only characters who actually utter the "F-word" or any other obscenities are a pair of drunken English soldiers.

SOCIAL ATTITUDES AND THE TV SCREEN

A now-dead member of the *Oireachtas* (Parliament) once famously claimed there had been no sex in Ireland before television. In a sense he had a point: the developing openness about sexuality in Ireland is a by-product television's challenging of social attitudes.

Irish television's *Late Late Show* provided a forum for debating the essential issues of Irish life for more than a generation, but but even more influential has been the widespread availability of British television through satellite and cable. The majority of Dublin households have been cabled for more than thirty years, and now most of the country is covered. These programs helped form the values of the under-forty generation—now a majority in the population.

chapter three

RELIGION &
TRADITION

THINGS ARE CHANGING

Catholic Ireland is an obviously religious country; there are shrines by the roadside, huge parking lots around the churches built to accommodate large crowds for Mass on Sundays, and many drivers in the Republic will cross themselves if they pass a church or a shrine.

When Pope John Paul II visited Dublin in 1979 he remarked that "On Sunday mornings in Ireland, no-one seeing the great crowds making their way to and from church could have any doubt about Ireland's devotion to the Mass."

In the seventies Sunday Mass attendance in Ireland was over 90 percent.But although in the 2011 census 3,681.000 stated that they were either Catholic or Catholic by birth, by 2012, weekly attendance at Mass had dropped to 35 percent and that figure was mostly made up of older people. Things had changed.

THE CATHOLIC CHURCH AND THE IRISH GOVERNMENT

The old unquestioning faith in the Catholic Church's moral authority was greatly strengthened with the coming of Irish independence and what the new regime was to call its "filial loyalty and devotion" to the Pope. But in the twenty-first century this governmental obsequiousness has been delivered a mortal blow by the scandals concerning pedophile priests and their cover up by the Church. In 2011 the *Taoiseach* Enda Kenny spoke in the *Dail* of the "dysfunction, disconnection, elitism . . . the narcissism that dominate the culture of the Vatican." He went on, "The delinquency and arrogance of a particular version . . . of 'morality' . . . will no longer be tolerated or ignored . . . . . Today, that Church needs to be a penitent Church, a Church truly and deeply penitent for the horrors it perpetrated, hid and denied."

NEW ATTITUDES

Even before these scandals came to light Irish men and women had become less willing to accept unquestioningly the Church's teaching on such matters as contraception. But in

2015 came the most indisputable proof that they are no longer in thrall to the Catholic Church. A nationwide referendum came down overwhelmingly in favor of gay marriage, in direct disobedience to the Church's teaching. Afterward Diarmuid Martin, Archbishop of Dublin, remarked "the Church needs to do a reality check." Significantly an earlier poll had found that

53 percent of those questioned said that religion was not an important aspect of their life. Even those who do believe are increasingly seeing belief as a personal matter.

It is important to acknowledge though that this drastic change of attitude is much more prevalent in the towns and cities than in rural areas of Southern Ireland. The Republic still has the highest percentage of regular churchgoers in Western Europe, and nearly 2,000 priests active in the parish. And nowadays active means active! No longer is the word of the priest law, but what he has to say still matters. This is partly because he is likely to be involved in all aspects of the life of his parish, including joining in the plays at the drama group or running the local dance— activities his predecessors would have castigated. Nor is today's Catholic priesthood hidebound: in a letter to the Bishops in June 2014 the Association of Irish Priests recommended an end to clerical celibacy and the ordination of women, at least as deacons, while a surprising number of clergy voted in favor of gay marriage in 2015 referendum.

RELIGIOUS FESTIVALS

Like other Catholic countries the Irish enjoy their religious festivals: colorful public ceremonies are held to mark the major festivals such as Easter, Pentecost, and the feast of Corpus Christi (on July 17), while visitors will often see young girls dressed as miniature brides for their "First Communion."

St. Patrick's Day

St. Patrick's Day (March 17) is still a religious

holiday in Ireland. While some of the razzmatazz that surrounds it in America has been exported to Ireland since the Republic declared it a "national festival" in the mid-nineties, do not expect green beer or the "kiss me, I'm Irish!" exuberance of the American experience. A get-together with friends or clubbing is more likely.

NORTHERN IRELAND

According to a 2007 survey, the North was the most religious part of Ireland, with 45 percent regularly attending church. Protestants and Catholics are equally devout. The two sides in the "Troubles" in Northern Ireland were largely defined by their religion: for better or worse, the separate identities of Republicans and the Loyalists in the Province still seem to be bound in with where their citizens pray on Sundays. But other religious communities are also represented which don't have political affiliations, including small Muslim, Hindu, Sikh, Buddhist, and Jewish communities.

Quo Vadis

Wherever they go in Ireland, but especially in the North and in rural areas in the South, visitors must understand that religion is still a hugely significant element in Irish cultural, domestic, and political life.

THE IRISH WAY OF DEATH

Irish attitudes toward death are quite different from those of the English. Mourning in Ireland is public and there is no shame in showing your feelings. You would be expected to commiserate with a friend or acquaintance, in the business world or elsewhere, who has suffered a recent loss.

Funerals are an important part of everyday life: food and drink are provided and everyone drinks to the memory of the departed. In the past, the custom known as "waking the dead" was for the body to remain in the house, and hours were spent sitting round the coffin, drinking, talking, and reminiscing. James Joyce took the title of his most notoriously difficult novel, *Finnegans Wake*, from a popular comic song about just such an event.

You will sometimes hear the expression "an American wake." In the old days when people emigrated to America there seemed little chance that they would ever see their friends and relatives again. They were passing out of their lives as if they were dying. So a wake was held for them.

And if the Irish derive such enjoyment from a time of grief, just imagine the fun of an Irish wedding!

THE CHURCH OF IRELAND

The Anglican "Church of Ireland" is a curious anomaly. When Henry VIII broke with Rome, the Irish Parliament passed a series of acts that ended the authority of the Pope over the Church in Ireland. Most of the bishops acquiesced, since the Celtic Irish Church had only surrendered its autonomy to Rome in the twelfth century. But in the reign of his daughter Elizabeth the first English Protestant prayer book was published, and in 1550 Ireland got its first printing press to print it. Then the troubles began.

The majority of Irish people spoke Gaelic, not English, so the book did not catch on. The Church split between those who stayed with the Latin Mass and were increasingly papist in sympathy and those, mostly the ruling classes, who adopted the Anglican rite. In brief, the Catholics got the vast bulk of the people, but the Anglicans got the churches and cathedrals, so the tradition of outdoor Masses for Catholics began. The weakness of the English administration in Ireland meant both Churches carried on in parallel.

Once the Irish forces supporting the Catholic King James II were beaten in 1690, the English rulers cracked down and penal laws were brought in to suppress not only Catholicism but the Presbyterians of the North. Catholic bishops and archbishops would not be officially allowed until Catholic emancipation in 1829. Since then there have been two sets of bishops across Ireland, the Roman Catholic and the Anglican. And as neither Church recognizes the border between the Republic and Northern Ireland both have dioceses that straddle it.

In September 2013 Pat Storey became the first female Anglican Bishop when she was appointed Bishop of Meath and Kildare in the Republic. The Church of Ireland has about 380,000 members North and South. In the Republic, more than in the fiercely nonconformist North, the 129,000 members of the Anglican community exercise an influence out of all proportion to their numbers. Many of Ireland's greatest writers and patriots came from this group.

ECUMENISM

Relations between the two denominations have been cordial since Independence in 1921. Both primates are based in Armagh in the North and they liaise closely, regularly appearing on television together to display solidarity in the face of sectarian prejudices and antagonisms. But sometimes the mischievous Irish sense of humor cannot be suppressed, even among all this mutual goodwill.

Danny Boy

Brendan Behan used to tell how the Bishop of Cork, the Most Reverend Doctor Daniel Cohalan—known affectionately as "Danny Boy"—lay in his last illness. He was old, over ninety, but his illness dragged on and on. It happened that the Protestant Bishop of Cork, a very much younger man, upped and died before him. A Monsignor brought the news to "Danny Boy" and stood around waiting for the words of spiritual consolation that he would convey to the Protestant chapter. There was a long silence. After a while, "Danny Boy" opened an eye, looked at the Monsignor and said to him: "Well, he knows now who's the real Bishop of Cork!"

THE PRESBYTERIAN CHURCH

The North has many nonconformist Protestant sects but the Presbyterian Church is the

dominant influence. It dates back to the
seventeenth-century "plantation" of Ulster
by Scottish Presbyterian settlers. Like the
Church of Scotland it has no bishops; instead
elected church members (elders) run each
individual congregation. The congregations
are grouped into Presbyteries, which ordain
ministers. Ministers and elders represent their
congregations at Presbytery and at regional
Synods. Overall control is in the hands of the
annual General Assembly, representing all 560
congregations in Ireland. Its chief representative
is the Moderator, who only serves for a single
year. The ministry has been open to women
since 1974 and in 2015 a woman was up for
election as the Moderator.

The Presbyterian Church has about 360,000
members, predominantly in the North.

METHODISTS AND OTHERS

The Irish Methodist Church has 234 churches, North and South, and 50,000 members. It was actively involved in promoting peace during the Troubles. Baptists, Congregationalists, Unitarians, and a wide variety of other sects (mainly in the North) number about 180,000 believers. Eire has 49,000 Muslims, but only 1,800 Jews—even though the "hero" of Ireland's most famous or notorious work of fiction, James Joyce's *Ulysses*, was a Jew. These communities are much smaller in Northern Ireland but nevertheless Belfast, like Dublin, has a mosque, a synagogue, a Sikh gurdwara, and several Hindu temples.

What to Wear

Visitors will be warmly welcomed in any place of worship. It is no longer necessary to dress in one's "Sunday best" and informality is now the general rule. If in doubt, a jacket and tie for males and the equivalent for females would ensure that you are not out of place.

THE RELIGIOUS ORDERS

There are over forty orders of monks and friars and fifty orders of nuns in Ireland: Carmelites, Fathers of the Holy Ghost, Augustinians, Capuchins, Dominicans, Marists, Oblates, Passionists, Franciscans, Jesuits, Redemptorists, and Vincentians to name just a few. The religious orders have a special if ambiguous place in the

Irish psyche, largely because so many people were educated by nuns or by the Christian Brothers, the Jesuits, or other orders.

Seamus Heaney once described the nuns of one particularly fashionable convent school as "The Little Sisters of the Rich." But though there were and are some such convents, there are many more "Little Sisters of the Poor," working with the disadvantaged of Ireland, or in hospitals. Fifteen years ago there were twelve and a half thousand people in religious orders. Today it is virtually impossible to get an overall figure but clearly there are significantly fewer—it has been reported that while 228 Irish nuns died in 2014 only two Irish women joined convents.

EDUCATION: EIRE

Many aspects of Irish life continue to be organized on denominational lines, especially education. The Catholic Church is the leading provider of education in the Republic, with 90 percent of all primary schools, while of the 723 secondary schools in Ireland, 376 "voluntary schools" are mostly run by the Catholic religious orders, with a few run by the Anglican Church of Ireland.

Most other schools are non-academic "vocational" schools, focusing on technical and professional training. All are publicly aided to provide free education (except a very few private schools). Students must study Gaelic, but examinations are no longer compulsory.

Education in the Republic is from ages five to sixteen, though many students stay on until eighteen to take the higher exams required for admission to university. The State meets almost all the cost of teachers' salaries.

There are nine universities: Trinity College, Dublin, University College Dublin , Maynooth University, Mary Immaculate College, Limerick University, University College Cork, the University of Limerick, the National University of Ireland, Galway, and Dublin City University, together with a number of other degree giving institutions such as the Royal College of Surgeons in Ireland and various technical institutes

EDUCATION: NORTHERN IRELAND

In Northern Ireland the basic system is the same as in the rest of the UK, with compulsory education from five to sixteen. There are GCSE (General Certificate of Secondary Education) examinations at sixteen, with Advanced Levels at eighteen for those who want to stay on, as many do. But in contrast to elsewhere in the UK, schooling is largely in the hands of the religious denominations, with 95 percent of pupils at all levels attending either a maintained (Catholic) school or a controlled school (mostly Protestant). The proportion of students in each type of school is roughly equal. Both are open to children of all faiths and none. Teaching a balanced view of some subjects can be difficult in these conditions, despite which Northern Ireland's results at GCSE and A-Level are consistently the best in the UK. There are some integrated schools, but only 14,000 pupils, or about 4 percent of the school population, attend them.

There are two universities, the Queen's University of Belfast and the University of Ulster, each with several campuses across the Province. Many Northern Irish students go to these in preference to colleges in mainland Britain. Often their time at university will be their first experience of mixing with members of a different religious community.

IRISH SAINTS

Ireland is full of local saints, including historical personages from the early centuries of Irish Christianity, miracle-workers who are said to have used their sacred power to banish monsters, cure illnesses, and provide food for the people in time of need. The best-known saints have a universal appeal and are part of the national consciousness.

St. Patrick

St. Patrick, the Patron Saint and Apostle of Ireland, is associated with the conversion of the country to the Celtic, as opposed to the Roman, form of Christianity in the fifth century. The son of a Romano-British official, he was carried off into slavery by Irish raiders as a child, and for some years tended sheep in Ulster. He escaped, trained for the priesthood, probably in France, and as a result of a dream, decided to return to Ireland. Tradition says that he arrived in 432 CE, at the age of forty-seven.

He landed in the north at Strangford Lough, and hastened off to the seat of the High King at Tara. There he won the royal family over by performing miracles that were vastly more

impressive than the magic of the local druids. Traditionally the shamrock became the symbol of Ireland when St. Patrick used it to demonstrate to the King of Munster the "three in one" nature of the Holy Trinity.

By the time he died, probably in 475, Patrick had ensured that most of Ireland was officially Christian. His last years were spent in Armagh, which is why Armagh is the seat of the Catholic and Protestant primates. As to where he is buried, the Book of Armagh simply states "Where his bones rest nobody knows."

St. Brigid

St. Brigid is the most popular saint in Ireland after Patrick. As protectress of farming and livestock she has many of the attributes of the ancient earth goddess. Her feast day is

significantly February 1,
the Celtic pagan festival of
Imbolc. It has rightly been
said that she symbolizes
the way Christianity did
not replace the old Celtic
tradition in Ireland but
rather was superimposed
on it.

Be that as it may,
Brigid is reputed to have
been born in County
Kildare in 457, where she
became a nun and performed many miracles.
There is a charming story that when a gold cross
was stolen from her convent she plaited rushes
to make a cross that would be equally holy but
otherwise worthless. On the eve of her festival
people still plait rushes to make crosses in her
name, and the Brigid's cross became one of the
symbols for Irish Television—which is not to
suggest that Irish Television is very holy but
otherwise worthless.

St. Brendan

St. Brendan the Navigator belongs to the mid-
sixth century, and was from Tralee in the south.
Among the monasteries he founded was Ardfert
near Tralee. It might have been even nearer
to Tralee had not the plans for the foundation
been seized by a crow, which flew off with them.
Brendan gave chase and where the crow dropped

the plans there he built his monastery. He is most famous for the *Navigio Sancti Brendani*, which describes how he and his monks sailed to

Iceland, Greenland, and possibly mainland America. In the 1970s Tim Severin demonstrated that the ancient Irish *currachs* of wood and leather were extremely seaworthy and could have sailed across the Atlantic. Other incidents in the book seem less likely—as when Brendan met Judas Iscariot having a brief holiday from Hell clinging to a rock, or when he celebrated his Easter Mass on the back of a whale.

St. Columba

St. Columba, usually known as *Colmcille* ("Colom-keel," Colum of the Church), was a great founder of monasteries, notably Durrow (est. 548), famous for its illuminated manuscripts. He caused a battle at Cul Dreimhne in 561 in which three thousand died, and in penance went off to Scotland where he founded another famous monastery on Iona and warded off the Loch Ness monster with the sign of the Cross.

PILGRIMAGE SITES

In many places holy wells, dedicated to individual saints, are still visited by pilgrims on their feast days, where the faithful pray to the saint for relief from physical and mental distress. In Synge's play *The Well of the Saints* a couple are cured of blindness at a holy well, and are distressed to find they are ugly and not beautiful as they imagined they were.

Other holy places are associated with St. Patrick: he is said to have banished snakes from Ireland standing on the summit of Croagh Patrick in Mayo. Each year thousands of pilgrims, quite a few barefoot, climb up its 2,510 feet (765 meters). In summer pilgrims go to Lough Derg (the Red Lake), where St. Patrick had a vision of Purgatory. For three days they follow the Stations of the Cross and eat one small meal a day.

At Knock, again in Mayo, in 1879 there were reports of the appearance of the Holy Family. But the bigger miracle is how a local parish priest got an enormous church (holding 20,000 people) built there and then persuaded the authorities to build an international airport!

GAELIC: THE ANCIENT IRISH LANGUAGE

Two thousand years ago much of Western Europe spoke some form of Celtic language. Irish is the oldest of the still-spoken Celtic tongues—Irish Gaelic, Scots Gallic, Welsh, and Breton—and like them has characteristics that seem strange to English speakers. For instance Gaelic is inflected at the start of words, not the end. So, for example, the word *bad* ("bard") means boat: "his boat" is "*a bad*," but "her boat" sounds completely different —"*a bhad*" ("vard")—and "their boat" is "*a mbad*" ("mard"), different again!

Regional Variation

Even with comparatively few people speaking Irish it still has several very distinct dialects. A native speaker from Connemara I came across thought Ulster Gaelic was a foreign language when he heard it on the radio!

By the mid-nineteenth century English was the dominant language in much of Ireland, but not so a hundred and fifty years before: even the Londonderry apprentice boys who yelled their defiance at James II and his Catholic army would have done so in Irish. In England Anglo-Saxon replaced the old Celtic language by the seventh century and in Irish the English are still known as "Saxons."

*Three things no man can trust: the hoof of a horse,
the horn of a bull, and the smile of a Saxon.*
(Translation of Gaelic proverb)

Irish is the earliest European language north
of the Alps in which extensive writings exist (see
"Mythology" below). The Gaelic alphabet was
developed from the Latin script
in the sixth century. Prior to this
the young bards were rigorously
trained to commit thousands of
lines to memory.

The British authorities actively
suppressed the use of Irish, and
for many people education went
on in illegal "hedge schools" scattered through the
countryside. In his play *Translations*, set in the early
nineteenth century, Brian Friel portrays one such
school. He also shows how, when the first Ordnance
Survey team arrived in Ireland to map the land, it
used local people to explain the Irish names, which
were then anglicized into the forms used today.

The Gaelic Revival

At the end of the nineteenth century, in 1893, the
Gaelic League (*Conradh na Gaelige*: "CONRA-na-
GAYLIGA") was founded to revive Irish speaking.
By then more than 85 percent of the population
spoke only English. Today Gaelic is the first language
of a small minority of people living in a few enclaves
on the western seaboard known as "the *Gaeltacht*"
("GAYL-takt"). Overall fewer than 50,000 people

speak Irish in preference to English, and the number grows smaller every year.

If few speak it fluently, more than a million people claim some proficiency in the language, including many living in the main cities. Basic Irish is still studied by the vast majority of children at school. Even if they do not use it in everyday life, many Irish people retain an attachment to the language and certain words and phrases still flavor everyday speech.

The Irish Care About Their Language

Foreigners are not expected to understand any Irish, but the visitor who does make even a minimal effort in this direction (for instance by being aware that the Prime Minister is known by his title of *Taoiseach* (pronounced "tee-shack") will gain disproportionately in goodwill. All the more so if you show an awareness that the Irish language is the repository of a marvellous literary tradition.

MYTHOLOGY

Although to their shame the English rulers ignored it, Ireland has the richest canon of recorded mythology of any northern country. Just as the Greeks are proud of and familiar with their mythology, so the Irish are proud of and familiar with theirs. Stories that were composed three centuries before Christ were passed on by generations of bards and written down by monks from the seventh century onward. Translated into English by Lady Augusta Gregory at the beginning of the twentieth century, they inspired the works of the great Irish writers of the period, especially Synge and Yeats, and were central to Ireland's rediscovery of its special identity and national pride.

Legendary Cycles

The legends have been collected into four cycles. The earliest is the Mythological Cycle, or *Book of Invasions*. This tells of the invasions of six races, of which the last three have traditionally been associated with various physical types still found in Ireland. These were the 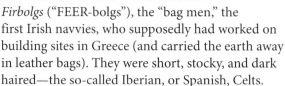 *Firbolgs* ("FEER-bolgs"), the "bag men," the first Irish navvies, who supposedly had worked on building sites in Greece (and carried the earth away in leather bags). They were short, stocky, and dark haired—the so-called Iberian, or Spanish, Celts.

A godlike people with magic cauldrons, magic spears, and the like, and a king with a silver hand, displaced the Firbolgs. They were the red-haired, green-eyed *Tuatha De Danann* ("TOO-ha jay DON-awn"), who were said to have originated the Druidic religion. They had strange powers, and even quite recently if fishermen saw a red-haired woman on the road they would turn back and refuse to put to sea.

But for all their magic the Tuatha De Danann were defeated by mortal men, the Milesians, or Gaels, "valiant, voluble, laughing and warlike, brown-haired, bright-eyed, skilled in the arts of peace and battle." The Tuatha De Danann were forced to live underground, coming out only at night. Ireland is full of Iron Age Barrows, or tumuli, and these were assumed to be the homes of the defeated magicians.

The Ulster Cycle originated sometime between the third and first centuries BCE. It includes famous characters like Fergus, the exiled King of Ulster, and Queen Maeve, the proud, scheming queen behind the Cattle Raid of Cooley. But above all it is the story of Cúchulainn ("coo-KHUL-in"), the champion of Ulster, who began life as a boy called Seftana. At the age of five he performed amazing heroic deeds and was seduced by hundreds of naked women. When he was six he killed the hound of Culann the Smith, and so had to take over the job of watchdog for

several years. Hence his nickname the "hound of Culann"—Cúchulainn. This cycle includes the story of Deirdre of the Sorrows, which Synge dramatized.

The Fenian Cycle seems to have been composed about 300 CE. By now a High King resides at Tara. The stories tell of Finn McCool, his war band, the Fianna, and his dog, Bran, who wander together all over Ireland.

Finn and the Fianna were hunting in the mountains of Donegal when a fog overcame them. Keen-eyed Diarmuid saw the white of a lime-washed cottage and there they found an old man and there was a sheep tied by the wall. The old man called to a woman below to bring food and a fine girl of exceeding beauty came and prepared a meal.

No sooner was the table laid than the sheep broke loose, upset the table and scattered the food. Finn told Conan to tie up the sheep again and Conan caught the sheep by the head. But he could not shift her though he used all his power. Then Diarmuid tried and every one of them, all without success.

The old man rose from the hearth and a multitude of ashes fell from his breeches as he hobbled to the sheep, seized it by the scruff and tied it up with ease.

A further meal was prepared and Finn went to the young girl for he had a great desire to lie with her. 'Finn McCool' she said, 'you had me once and you won't have me again.' Then all the company tried but all had the same answer.

At length the girl explained. For the name of the sheep was Strength itself and it was stronger than any warrior, but the old man was Death and Death will overcome strength. And the girl herself was called 'Youth,' which all had had once but none would ever have again.

(Translated from the Fenian Cycle)

Finn's son Oisin and his nephew Caoilte were the only survivors of the Fianna. In old age Oisin supposedly met St. Patrick, and it is this meeting that Yeats celebrates in his *Wanderings of Oisin*.

Finally, the Historical Cycle includes legendary stories of real people and is heavily Christianized. It stretches from the third century BCE to Brian Boru, the High King who defeated the Vikings in the eleventh century.

IRISH FAIRY LORE

Ireland is famous for its fairy lore, which contains vestiges of pre-Christian traditions. In Irish, fairies are known as *sidhe* (pronounced "shee"), a word that originally designated a mound or tumulus. In the Mythological Cycle it is recorded that, after the Milesians defeated the Tuatha De Danann, this magical race retreated from human sight beneath the ground where they became the *sidhe* and lived in *Tir Na Nog* ("Cheer na nohg"), the land of perpetual youth.

So the Tuatha De Danann became "the people" (never "the little people," many were pretty big) as the Irish called the fairies. And these highly resentful former rulers of the island are anything but charming.

The *Bean-sidhe* ("BANshee:" woman of the fairy) can be a young woman, a stately matron, or an old hag, or she might be a hare, a crow, or some other magic animal. Her wailing gives notice of death.

The *Pooka* ("POOK-ah") is often a dark horse with flowing mane and smoldering eyes that takes its riders, frequently drunks, on wild rides by night. In County Down he is a goblin—and there several sheaves of corn would be left standing at the end of the harvest as "the pooka's share."

The *Leprechaun* ("LEP-ruckh-awn"), who has unaccountably come to stand for all Irish fairies, is a *Leath Bhrogan*, a maker of brogues, a shoemaker. He has a red coat with seven buttons in each row and is usually drunk. The Leprechauns took it upon themselves to guard the treasure looted by the Danes, which they store in crocks, or pots. Catch one and you may get him to hand over his crock of gold, or at least mend your shoes.

The *Moruadh* ("Merrow") wears a red cap and lives beneath the sea. Fishermen in some areas see her as a messenger of death, though several families claim Merrows among their ancestors.

Other delightful fairy-folk are the *Dullaghan* ("DULLA-han"), who, headless or carrying his head, rides a black coach and throws a bowl of blood over you to tell you that you are going to die; and the *Leanaun-Shee* ("LAN-awn shee"), who likes to mate with human males. Refuse one and she will become your slave, accept her and you will become her slave and waste away, unless you can find someone to take your place as her lover.

chapter four

MAKING FRIENDS

GETTING ON WITH THE IRISH

There is a magic about Ireland, in the people and the culture, but do not hope to find it at every turn. Reality, most of the time, is as ordinary here as elsewhere. Young Irish people are as likely to have a degree-level education as anyone else in the English-speaking world. These days they are more likely to work on a computer than on a farm (60 percent of the population live in towns and cities. The Irish have access to the same range of goods and services, eat the same fast food, and watch the same movies and TV as everyone else does.

Nonetheless, old-fashioned values still matter. And none more than good manners. As one businessman remarked, "Good manners are good business—you don't get a second chance to make a good impression."

There is even evidence that companies are relocating to Ireland because they appreciate the warm and friendly manner. "English people tend to be more formal. They say the right thing but come across as cold." And the Irish expect the same good manners from the people they deal with.

Manners Makyth Money

With regard to doing business in Ireland, Lisa Muza Grotts, the director of a major consultancy firm says categorically, "It all comes down to "please," "May I?" "I am sorry," "Excuse me," and "Thank you." Each time you omit one of these terms you are hurting feelings and profits.

Greeting in Ireland is generally by handshake, although the continental habit of kissing ladies on the cheek has made inroads in some circles. The Irish tend to be stiffer about physical contact than, say, the Latins, but a foreigner, especially if not English, is generally expected to be a bit more flamboyant in these matters.

Personal relations are fairly informal: more in line with American or Australian norms than North European practice. People like to get on first-name terms from the beginning. Friendships are formed quickly and visitors often find themselves invited to meet friends, or perhaps to play a round of golf or tennis.

Providing they do not stand on ceremony, foreigners will be quickly drawn into a typical rapid-fire conversation spiced with humor and imagination, though they must still be prepared sometimes to be the object of curiosity in a few remote country areas.

HOME LIFE

Houses and apartments in both town and country are generally modern and well appointed. Neither the picturesque thatched cottage nor the rambling great house is likely to be someone's home nowadays, and Dublin's remaining lovely Georgian terraces usually house prestigious offices rather than families. Home life is much the same as elsewhere in the Western world, with the same comforts and facilities.

The Irish are neighborly and hospitable. Dropping by, without a prior telephone call, is accepted practice, and informal social events are not uncommon. Standing on ceremony or dressing up to call on friends would be seen as pretentious.

Because they are by nature hospitable the Irish are much more likely to invite you into their home than are the English. Should you be invited, given the high cost of alcohol in Ireland, a bottle of wine or spirits makes a welcome gift.

Get the Timing Right!

Irish social events tend to run later than in America or Britain. Guests at a dinner party, for example, will not be expected to arrive precisely on time. On the other hand, leaving well before midnight could be interpreted by your hosts as a sign that their party has been deemed by you to be a failure.

Country Time

In fact, the Irish generally still tend to be quite laid back about time. When a friend of mine asked when the buses came along in a rural district he got the reply, "Oh every so often with a few gaps in between."

On the subject of timing, an arrangement to meet at a pub at a particular time can be interpreted flexibly. Be warned: a delay of anything up to three quarters of an hour is not unusual.

The Irish attitude toward children resembles that of southern Europe. Children are accepted at social events, and if they make a nuisance of themselves it causes less concern than in some other countries. Families were relatively large until quite recently, but fewer than two children are the norm.

Increasingly both partners have jobs, so the pattern of family life is rapidly becoming much the same as elsewhere in the West, especially among younger people.

chapter five

CULTURAL LIFE

MUSIC, SONG, AND DANCE

The Irish love to dance, and Irish dance is central to Irish culture. Now, thanks to *Riverdance* and *Lord of the Dance*, it has traveled the world, but as to where it all started that, as with so much else in Ireland, is shrouded in the mists of myth and make-believe. Certainly Irish dancing was well established by the sixteenth century, when beautiful and beautifully dressed Galway girls dancing jigs impressed Sir Philip Sidney. To this day Irish dancing, unlike Scottish dancing, is chiefly the role of the womenfolk.

"Step-dancing" is essentially individual showing off. It began in competitions between dancing masters in the eighteenth century. The trick is to dance on one spot—you are supposed to be able to "dance on a plate," keeping your legs together, your hands to your sides, your face expressionless, and making as much noise as possible, with the immensely complicated footwork striking the floor known as "battering." There are step-dancing competitions all over Ireland.

A *Ceili* ("KAY-lee") is essentially a party, though one at which you might be asked to sing a song or

perform in some other way. In the old days a whole
neighborhood would get together to dance, play
music, and tell stories. Ceili dancers dance on their
toes, extending legs and feet, rather than battering
the floor with them.

"Set dances" are rather like square dances, and
seem to have evolved from an old French dance—
the quadrille. In summer the young people would
meet up and dance at the crossroads to the music
of a fiddle. Set dances involve four couples and have
enormous regional variations. The Catholic Church
tried to use the Public Dance Hall Act of 1935 to
stamp them out, and they were only accepted into
the canon of Irish dance in the 1950s.

The *ard fheis* ("ARD-esh") or dance festival is
the best place to see Irish dancing, and there are
hundreds all over Ireland. Costumes are supposed
to be based on peasant dress, and those of the
women are often covered in beautiful hand-

embroidered Celtic designs. The men's costumes have a vaguely Scottish look with a saffron-colored kilt, short jackets, and a folded cloak draped over the shoulder.

TRADITIONAL MUSIC

Dance needs music, and much Irish traditional instrumental music has its origins in the dance—in jigs, reels, polkas, hornpipes, and such. If today dance has become a little institutionalized, music remains vastly more informal; in pubs all over Ireland, but especially in the west, you can hear players of a surprisingly high general standard. In essence the tradition of Irish music and song is oral rather than written—it is passed on from player to player, singer to singer.

Irish music has been called "a living popular tradition," so much so that people forget who wrote which song. Indeed the long tradition of

anonymous songs stretches back into the past, or at least into the eighteenth and nineteenth centuries. Tunes are adapted, frills are added, meters change, and alternative versions of the words proliferate. Dominic Behan once discovered songs he had written appearing in songbooks as "Anon. Traditional."

MUSICAL STYLES

The best-known Irish instruments are probably the small Irish harp, which has long been a national symbol (and even achieved the accolade of being adopted by Guinness as their trademark), and the *Uilleann* ("ILL-in") or elbow pipes, which are worked by bellows and have a quieter, more mellow sound than Scottish pipes. Both were originally aristocratic

instruments—the pipes were far too expensive for the ordinary laborer. At one point there seemed a possibility that they would disappear, but today there are probably more Irish pipers than ever before. Ironically the version normally played was developed in Philadelphia.

For ordinary folk the most popular instruments were the fiddle (or violin) and various forms of accordion and concertina. Nowadays guitars, of course, appear everywhere, but so do mandolins and, especially, banjos, which were brought over from America and lost one of their five strings on the voyage.

Wind instruments are the old wooden flute and the humble tin whistle (a simple metal tube with six holes and a mouthpiece like a recorder), which in the hands of accomplished players like James Galway can achieve an amazing virtuosity.

The two uniquely Irish percussion instruments are the *Bodhran* ("BOR-arn") and the Lambeg drum. The *Bodhran* is a round frame with a goatskin stretched over it, played with a double-ended baton that produces a stirring rapid rattle. Though apparently traditional it first appeared in the late 1950s. The Lambeg is much older and is uniquely associated with Northern Protestants. It is a huge drum weighing 33 pounds (15 kg) that is carried in Orange processions and whipped rather than beaten. It can be heard for miles.

Marching bands are indeed a characteristic of the North, and both the Protestant and Catholic communities have bands that accompany their parades and processions.

Music Takes Sides

The two sides in Northern Ireland were divided by their music and their songs. One of the best-known Northern Irish Protestant songs tells the story of the "Ould Orange Flute," whose owner converted to Catholicism, but the flute refused to play any but Protestant music until in the end it was burned at the stake by the priests as a heretic. Similarly many of the traditional Irish songs that are known throughout the world and through which Irish people expressed their feelings and aspirations often have a republican theme: songs like The "Bold Fenian Men", or "Kevin Barry" date back to the early twentieth century and well beyond.

But there were also the showbands that flourished from the fifties to the early seventies and had nothing to do with traditional instruments, tunes, or politics. These were touring dance bands playing cover versions of rock and roll, standard dance numbers, Dixieland jazz, and Country and Western. Today Irish music is a rich mix of many influences, often combining traditional and modern forms. It has become international in the hands of world-class pop performers like Van Morrison, U2, Sinead O'Connor, or the Corrs, and in the virtuoso performances of The Chieftains.

LITERATURE AND THE BARDIC TRADITION

Visitors are often surprised at how interested in, and knowledgeable about, poetry and drama the ordinary people of Ireland are. Irish literature is an accepted part of normal everyday experience. It may have something to do with the role literature played in Ireland's reassertion of its own identity, or simply the Irish love of language (in old Gaelic society every chieftain had his bard, and the villages had *seanchies*: traveling storytellers).

Until the late seventeenth century Irish literature meant literature in the Gaelic language. Bardic schools trained poets, *fili* ("Fillee"), to compose elaborate Gaelic verses. The brutal wars of the period brought this world to an end. The last, and one of the greatest, of the bards was Thurlough O'Carolan (1670–1738). It was said that at his funeral ten harpists vied to play laments for his passing.

About this time Brian Merriman was born in Limerick. An obscure schoolmaster, in 1780 he wrote one of the most notable Gaelic poems. *Midnight Court* is a fine, bawdy, anticlerical, and feminist tale in which the poet is abducted to a court presided over by the beautiful fairy queen, Aiobheal, where women arraign men for their sexual shortcomings.

Otherwise the eighteenth century belongs to the Anglo-Irish writers, and it is surprising how many of the major English-language writers were Irishmen. Almost the only eighteenth-century playwrights whose work is still performed are

George Farquhar (1678–1707), author of *The Recruiting Officer* and *The Beaux' Stratagem*, Oliver Goldsmith (1728–74), author of *She Stoops to Conquer*, and Richard Brinsley Sheridan (1751–1816), who wrote *The Rivals*, *The School for Scandal*, and *The Critic*. All three were Irish Protestants, and Farquhar and Goldsmith were educated at the Protestant Trinity College, Dublin.

So, too, was the satirist Jonathan Swift (1667–1747), Dean of St. Patrick's Cathedral, author of *Gulliver's Travels* (1726), and probably the most famous prose writer of the period. Maria Edgeworth (1767–1849) was one of the first women novelists, and her *Castle Rackrent* was an attack on the Irish landlord class to which she belonged. Inevitably most of these writers came to England to make their mark.

If Irish Protestant playwrights enlivened the eighteenth-century stage, so they did that of the late nineteenth and early twentieth centuries. Oscar Wilde (1854–1900) was the son of a Dublin surgeon and attended Trinity College before going to Oxford: *The Importance of Being Earnest* is arguably the finest English comedy of manners ever written—it is certainly the most successful. George Bernard Shaw (1856–1950) was brought up in a Dublin back street. The son of a drunken wastrel father, he left school at fifteen to work for an estate agent. At twenty he fled with his mother to England, where he wrote a string of dramas for the stage, most of which are still frequently performed. He won the Nobel Prize in 1925.

The Gaelic League

However, while Wilde and Shaw were making their names in England, great things were happening in Ireland. With the foundation of the Gaelic League in 1893, intended to assert the Irishness of the Irish people, came an enthusiasm not just for the Irish language but for Irish dance, Irish poetry and song, Irish sports, Irish mythology, even Irish clothing. Its moving spirit was a delightful man called Douglas Hyde, the son of a Protestant clergyman and another Trinity College graduate.

It would be hard to overestimate the importance of the Gaelic League on the future of Ireland, even though it was founded by middle-class Protestant intellectuals. Michael Collins, as hardheaded a man of action as ever Ireland produced, called it the "greatest event . . . in the whole history of the nation," since it "did more than any other movement to restore the national pride, honor, and self respect."

Hyde went on to become Professor of Modern Irish, a concept that could not have existed without him, at University College, Dublin, and, much to his own surprise, first President of the Irish Republic. His genius lay in reclaiming not just Gaelic literature but the poetry of the proverbs and everyday speech of the Irish countryman.

Above all it was William Butler Yeats (1865–1939), the grandson of a Protestant clergyman, whose work inspired this Irish renaissance. In his own poetry and plays Yeats, who was awarded the Nobel Prize for Literature in 1923, drew heavily on the Irish mythological past and so made the Irish people aware and proud of the richness of their birthright.

Yeats also got together with other idealists, like Lady Augusta Gregory, the widow of an Anglo-Irish landowner, to form the Irish National Theatre Society. In 1907 they opened the Abbey Theatre in Dublin with *The Playboy of the Western World* by John Millington Synge. While Synge's background was similar to theirs, he had lived on the Aran Islands and managed to capture the speech and culture of the islanders. Because it did not romanticize them, *The Playboy* caused an uproar on the first night.

Yeats and Lady Gregory belonged to the Celtic Revival, or "Celtic Twilight" as it was sometimes called, and wrote plays set in the mythological past. But the Abbey's real future lay elsewhere. Sean O'Casey was also a Protestant, but otherwise very different from the "Celtic Twilight" group.

He had worked as a laborer, was a convinced socialist, and had been a member of the rebel Irish Citizens Army. His great Dublin Trilogy— *The Shadow of a Gunman*, *Juno and the Paycock*, and *The Plough and the Stars*—was about the Easter Rising, the "Tan War," and the Civil War. Though put on by the Abbey in the 1920s when wounds were still raw, they pulled no punches in condemning the men of violence on both sides and speaking out for compassion. The plays are full of humor but their message is the stuff of tragedy. As Juno prays when she learns her son has been executed by his comrades, "Blessed Virgin, where were you when me darlin' son was riddled with bullets? Sacred heart of Jesus, take away our hearts o' stone and give us hearts o' flesh!" It was a line much quoted in Northern Ireland in the seventies and eighties.

Juno was hissed when it was first performed, and there was a full-scale riot when *The Plough and the Stars* dared to criticize the Easter Rising— whose banner pictured a plough and stars.

The Gate, Micheal Mac Liammoir's theater, founded in 1928, staged European classics, but The Abbey continued to mount controversial plays into the 1950s, with Brendan Behan's *The Hostage*, about the IRA, of which he had been a member, and later with Tom Murphy's *The Famine* (1964). More recently it maintained its reputation for realistic, unromantic pictures of Irish life with Billy Roche's trilogy about his home town of Wexford, and for controversy with

John Breen's *Hinterland*, a thinly disguised attack on the former Prime Minister Charles Haughey.

Across Ireland there is an enthusiasm for theater with numerous drama festivals and local groups: John B. Keane lived in the little town of Listowel in County Kerry: his plays, such as *Big Maggie*, which went to Broadway, and *The Field*, which became a major film, were premiered by an amateur group in Cork.

IRISH NOVELISTS

Of the hundreds of Irish novelists there is room to mention only a few. Edna O'Brien's *Country Girls* trilogy draws on her experience of being brought up in an "enclosed, fervid, and bigoted" village and educated in a convent. With his recent death John McGahern has been recognized as a major figure. His novels, too, reflect his own experience, and for years *The Dark* was banned in Ireland for its unflattering picture of the priesthood. The hugely popular Maeve Binchy (died 2012) was equally at home writing about village life and about young Irish women in London, and Roddy Doyle's novels about life on a Dublin housing estate combine popular appeal with a serious analysis of Irish society.

Distinguished younger writers include Colm Toibin, Claire Keegan, and Colum McCann, and, above all, Anne Enright, the winner of the Booker Prize in 2007 and appointed the first Irish Fiction Laureate in 2015. Unlike the other younger writers she is still resident in Ireland. She also belongs to a fine tradition of short story writers, which includes Frank O'Connor, Sean O'Faolain, and William Trevor.

Flann O'Brien wrote equally well in English and Irish. His comic English-language masterpieces, *At Swim Two Birds* and *The Third Policeman*, are among the few works worthy of comparison with *Ulysses*.

Which brings up James Joyce. *Ulysses*, published in1922, is probably the most influential novel ever written. Every chapter is in a different style as, in imitation of the travels of Odysseus in Homer's *Odyssey*, it traces the travels of Leopold Bloom around Dublin on a single day in 1904.

Samuel Beckett worked with Joyce, and his plays, of which the most famous is *Waiting for Godot*, have had the same profound effect on theatrical writing across the world as Joyce has had on prose.

The Northern Renaissance

The Milesians, having conquered the Tuatha de Danaan, sent a harpist south and a bard to the north. And to this day, it is sometimes claimed, the musicians hail from the South and the poets and writers from the North.

Though this is debatable, there has been an amazing flowering of literature in the North. First came the poet Louis MacNeice, then in the sixties a galaxy of talent emerged, including the novelist Maurice Leitch and the playwright Brian Friel, held by many to be among the greatest living dramatists, and the poets Michael Longley, Derek Mahon, and Seamus Heaney. The son of a small farmer, Heaney was Boyston Professor of Rhetoric and Poetry at Harvard and Professor of Poetry at Oxford; in 1995 he was awarded the Nobel Prize for Literature. He died in 2013.

These were followed by a second wave of younger writers, the poets Tom Paulin, Ciaran Carson, and Paul Muldoon, and the playwrights, Stewart Parker, Ann Devlin, and Gary Mitchell.

FILM

The 1990s saw a series of films about Ireland, starting with *The Field* in 1991. Many had themes based on the Troubles: films like *Patriot Games*, with Harrison Ford, *Some Mother's Son*, and *Cal* with Helen Mirren. Others were simply about life in Ireland, like the film version of Maeve Binchy's *Circle of Friends*, *Widows Peak* with Mia Farrow, set in the 1920s, and the delightful homegrown comedy *Waking Ned Divine*, about a dead lottery winner and a whole village of schemers.

Since the year 2000 there has been a further spate of films around the Troubles in the North: *Bloody Sunday*, *Trapped*, *Fifty Dead Men Walking*, *Five Minutes of Heaven*, *Hunger*, and, above all, *71* (2014). Most of these films were not actually Irish productions but *Calvary,* also 2014, was, and concerns the effect of child abuse by priests, not on an evil priest but a good one.

FESTIVALS

Poetry in Irish and English, drama, jazz, film, dance, and traditional music are all good excuses for a festival or *feis* ("FESH") or *Flea cheoil* ("FLAH hyowl"—a music festival), and Ireland has an awful lot of festivals, many of which seem to take place in Galway. Here is a small selection:

January: Shannonside Winter Music Week; Temple Bar Tradfest Dublin

February: Castlereagh Verbal Arts Festival; *Éigse na Brídeoige*, Irish cultural festival, Kerry; Spring Festival, Belfast

March: St. Patrick's Day (17th); Limerick International Band Festival; Dublin Film Festival

April: Cuirt International Festival of Poetry and Literature

May: *Flea na gCuach* ("FLAH-na-Guarch"), the Cuckoo festival, Kinvara; Ericsson All Ireland Drama Festival; Early Music Festival in Galway; Blues in the Bay Festival at Warren Point; Belfast Film Festival; Dublin Dance Festival

June: Cork Midsummer Festival; International

Organ and Choral Festival, Dublin; Bloomsday Festival (16th)— the day in 1904 when James Joyce sent Leopold Bloom wandering round Dublin in *Ulysses*; Wexford Literary Festival; Clonmel Junction Festival

July: Galway Arts Festival; *Fleadh Cheoil na Mumhan*, Killarney; Ballyshannon Folk and Traditional Music Festival

August: All Ireland Dance Festival; Wagner Festival, Limerick; "Gathering of the boats" at Kinvara; "Rose of Tralee"; Puck Fair, Killorglin

September: Lisdoonvarna Matchmaking Festival; Dublin Jazz Festival; Dublin Theatre Festival; Galway Oyster Festival; Waterford Harvest Festival

October: Wexford Opera Festival; Cork Guinness Jazz Festival; Belfast Festival at Queen's University

November: Drogheda Traditional Music Weekend; Ennis Tradfest; Cashel Arts Festival

December: Winter Solstice Festival, Newgrange

The Puck Fair merits a touch more detail. It is a totally pagan occasion that takes place on three successive days in August, generally the 10th, 11th, and 12th, at Killorglin on the River Laune. The three days are known as Gathering Day, Binding Day, and Scattering Day. The key event, and what makes the whole thing so outrageously pre-Christian, is the crowning with flowers of a very obviously male, or puck, goat on the first day in the presence of 30,000 celebrating spectators.

chapter **six**

TIME OUT

FOOD AND EATING OUT

The Irish diet is broadly similar to that of Britain.
Continental Europe has exercised an increasing
influence and, as in Britain, has done much
to bring about a new focus on quality, choice,
and service.

Restaurants and Pub Food

Nothing symbolizes the transformation of Irish life
in the last thirty years more than the proliferation
of restaurants and eating establishments of all
kinds, many noted for their high quality and some
for equally high prices.

In Dublin it is possible to sample most of the
world's cuisines. Temple Bar, Dame Street, and
the Grafton Street and Duke Street areas are
particularly rich in restaurants. Mexican, Italian,
and Indian can all be found, as well as fine seafood
restaurants; Chinese restaurants abound, as do
chains of kebab and Middle Eastern food shops.
There are even, despite the Irish fondness for meat,
plenty of vegetarian restaurants.

For local dishes and fine plain cooking, Irish
pubs offer good food and good value, especially

at lunchtime. One of the most famous Dublin pubs is Davy Byrne's in Duke Street—famous because it appears in James Joyce's *Ulysses*. In a typically "Joycean" passage, Leopold Bloom drops into Davy Byrne's for a sandwich of gorgonzola cheese and mustard, washed down with a glass of Burgundy.

> *Mr Bloom ate his strips of sandwich, fresh clean bread, with relish of disgust, pungent mustard, the feety savour of green cheese. Sips of his wine soothed his palate. Not logwood that. Tastes fuller this weather with the chill off . . . .*
> (James Joyce, *Ulysses*)

Incidentally, Irish pubs, like New York bars, are usually named after the proprietor. The oldest pub in Dublin is called "The Brazen Head," but such fanciful names are rare. Belfast pubs are much the

same, though an exception is "The Crown," a pub so visually stunning that it is owned by the Arts Council!

Continental-style cafés are mushrooming in towns throughout the island, contributing to the evolution of a whole new lifestyle. Most serve light food, and some serve alcohol as well.

Traditional Irish breakfasts include bacon, egg, sausage, tomatoes, white and black puddings (made from pig's blood), soda and potato bread, all followed by toast and washed down with tea. If you are staying at a farmhouse, with luck, everything will be local produce. If you are staying in town, remember the Irish are not famous for being early risers, so that by the time your breakfast arrives you will probably be hungry enough to eat it.

In Dublin, with the spread of health consciousness among the growing middle class, the norm is now likely to be a light breakfast and a snack lunch with the main meal in the evening.

English-style afternoon tea has never really been part of Irish life, though some hotels do serve it. In Northern Ireland, however, "High Tea," served from about 5:30 p.m. onward, is something very special and frequently the main meal of the day. There is tea, of course, but with it come scones, cakes, several types of bread, including currant or raisin bread, cold meat or a hot dish, a grilled or fried fish. Sometimes Ulster hotels do not even serve dinner in the evening, and where they do it can be expensive.

In the Republic, at least in the towns, you should have no trouble finding restaurants that serve evening meals, and many pubs serve them. Be warned though, that these places can close quite early, and pubs in particular are often unwilling to serve food after 8:30 or 9:00 p.m. when the bartenders want to get down to their proper business of selling drinks.

Sundays

The explosion of fast-food restaurants means you can eat cheaply most hours of the day or night in the Republic. Basic shopping on a Sunday is rarely a problem either, as the southern Irish do not have a rigid Sabbatarian culture (Irish games, for example, are played on Sundays). Be warned though, the same is not true of Northern Ireland. In Northern Ireland pubs used be shut on Sundays but are now open with limited opening hours. Going out to a restaurant for Sunday lunch is something of an institution, and since comparatively few places are open it is always advisable to book. Many restaurants that open Sunday lunchtime are closed in the evening.

Service

Away from the fast-food outlets service can be leisurely. And unfortunately attempting to hurry the Irish waiter or waitress can be counterproductive. Not that they will argue with you. If you complain they will apologize and find some plausible excuse. But the resentment at what they see as your impatience can come out in making you wait even longer. The Irish themselves, while they may grumble privately, tend to suffer in silence.

TIPPING

There is not a strong tipping culture in Ireland but tipping is expected in hotels and restaurants, with 10–15 percent being the norm. The percentage charge to the check has been introduced in some establishments, leaving no need to tip.

If you are buying drinks in Irish pubs, except possibly where you are seated at a table and there is a waiter, you should not leave a tip. The English practice of offering the bar staff a drink is not widespread either.

Generous Portions, Loaves and Fishes, and of course Potatoes

The glory of Irish country food is the quality of local produce, and it is always worth sampling local specialities like Limerick ham or Galway oysters (served with buttered brown bread and Guinness).

Salmon, fresh or smoked locally, and local lamb are the other famous specialities of the west. Irish beef is generally excellent, though if you want it rare make sure to ask specially for an "underdone" steak since the Irish do tend to cook food rather longer than is the custom elsewhere in Europe. In the winter season game and venison are also very good.

Old habits die hard and everywhere in rural Ireland no meal is complete without a serving of potatoes. Indeed, food often comes with two different forms of potato. Boiled potatoes, usually in their skins, will be served together with roasted potatoes, mashed potatoes, or even French fries.

Except in the main urban centers salads are generally unimaginative and disappointing—though like so much else in Ireland, tastes are changing rapidly.

Irish portions tend to be generous. Generosity (in Irish *flathuil* –"FLA-hooal") is a much-admired trait in Irish life—even in international hotels—but no offense will be taken if food is left.

All too often now you are served standard sliced bread. Yet proper Irish bread is world-famous, and Northern Irish bread is regarded throughout Ireland as the best of all. Soda bread

is made of stone-ground wheat flour baked on a griddle, and, instead of yeast, bicarbonate of soda and buttermilk are used. "Baps" are usually soft rolls, while "bannocks" are a soda bread made from oatmeal, which were originally Scottish. "Barmbrack" is a spiced bread served at high tea—and, of course, there is potato bread.

Freshwater fish, notably excellent salmon and trout, have always been a valued part of the Irish menu, but until quite recently this was not the case with seafood, which many people thought "rots the brain."

Today, though, seafood is an Irish speciality, and especially in the west. Fine West Coast lobsters, scallops, mussels, and sole can all be found in the restaurants of Galway or exported to those of Dublin, and they are generally simply and deliciously cooked.

Knives and Forks

Table manners in Ireland follow the English convention of holding the knife in the right hand and the fork in the left. The American practice of changing the fork over to the right hand to eat with after the food has been cut up is not usual.

IRISH DISHES

While Ireland has not evolved as comprehensive a cuisine as, say, France or Italy, or even, let's face it, Malta, there are distinctive dishes well worth trying. These, of course, usually involve potatoes.

"Boxty" is a sort of potato pancake using both mashed and ordinary boiled potatoes (sometimes with an egg added) fried in bacon fat.

"Colcannon" is mashed potato incorporating cabbage and onion. A simpler version called "Champ" is mashed potato with spring onions.

"Dublin Coddle" is a sort of thick stew in which sausages and bacon are interlayered with onions and, yes, potatoes, cooked in a ham stock.

It should not be confused with Irish stew, which is made with cheap cuts of lamb, carrots, onions, potatoes and any other root vegetables available, plus pearl barley.

"Bacon and Cabbage" is just that—and delicious if the bacon is home-cured and the cabbage is not overcooked.

Finally, to bring us on to drinks, two dishes involving Guinness. Beef in Guinness is Ireland's answer to *coq au vin*, and Guinness Cake is a rich fruitcake additionally flavored with Guinness.

DRINKING AND PUBS

The pub is the great focus of Irish social life. In the countryside the pub sometimes doubles as the local grocer's shop and, with the church, is the center of village life. The Irish pub, whether in the great cities, in towns, or in the countryside, is

an egalitarian place where all classes and nationalities can mingle and enjoy the art of conversation over a few drinks. There is an easiness, a sense of bonhomie that, quite apart from the drink, can prove intoxicating.

In Dublin restaurants and pubs there is as good a selection of wines available as there was in 1904 when Mr. Bloom drank his glass of Burgundy in Davy Byrne's. But elsewhere, particularly in rural areas, this is not always the case.

Unlike England, Ireland does not produce a great number of local beers. There are two drinks, however, that are specifically Irish, and ordering these will earn you your host's approval.

One is whiskey. The Irish insist that the first whiskey (which they spell with an "e") was Irish, not Scotch. The word is a corruption of the Gaelic *uisce beatha*, which means "water of life," and this, they say, was invented by Irish monks in the sixth century. Certainly the world's oldest (legal) distillery is at Bushmills on the Antrim coast, where they have been making whiskey since 1608.

Each Irish whiskey has a distinct taste, so people tend to order their favorite by name. Apart from Bushmills, other well-known whiskeys are John Jameson of Dublin, John Powers and Paddy of Cork, and Locke's of  Kilbeggan. Tullamore Dew, which has a sweeter, smoother taste, is often drunk as an aperitif.

Poteen

They might not admit it but some of these distillers had their origin in the illegal distilling of *poteen* ("po-cheen"), a clear, very alcoholic spirit. In the early nineteenth century there were said to be 2,000 illicit distillers in Ireland, though I've no idea who counted them. There are indeed still plenty of illegal poteen makers in the countryside, but it is not recommended that you try their wares. If you are desperate to taste poteen, the law was changed in 1997 to enable it to be brewed legally, so legal, hygienically distilled poteen is now available in some liquor stores.

Then there is Irish coffee—hot, sweet, black coffee with a good measure of Irish whiskey and

topped with whipped cream. Though not exactly an ancient Irish tipple—it is said to have been invented by a barman at Shannon airport in the 1950s—still a luxurious ending to any meal.

But it is Guinness, a brand of black beer made with dark roasted barley, that is synonymous with Ireland around the world. It is seen as the national drink—though in fact there are other, similar, dark beers. Beamish and Murphy's, for instance, both have devoted followings.

In Ireland you may hear Guinness called "porter" or "stout." Porter was invented not in Ireland but in London. It got its name from being drunk by porters, and was a particularly cheap beer that used dark roasted barley to cover up any imperfections drifting in the glass. Many of the porters who drank it were Irish Catholics, so the idea got back to Dublin where in 1759 Arthur Guinness took over an abandoned brewery in St. James' Gate. In Dublin "porter" was later called "plain" to distinguish it from proper Guinness.

Later, hearing of a much improved version that the porters at London's Covent Garden market had taken to drinking, Arthur Guinness tried his hand at this stronger, or "stout" version. So, just as "Scotch whisky" was invented in Ireland, so the origin of Ireland's favorite beverage is actually London, England!

Soon Guinness spread all over the world, and the Guinness family became a force to be reckoned with in Irish Society. They were especially involved in charitable work.

The Goodness of Guinness

When the writer Brendan Behan became famous he was taken up by the Guinness family. One day they were discussing the good works the family had done, and one of them said to the writer, "The Guinness family have done a lot for the people of Ireland." "True," said Brendan, "but that's nothing to what the people of Ireland have done for the Guinness family!"

To watch an Irish barman carefully pouring a draught Guinness can be quite an experience. It may take up to five minutes, after which it is smoothed off with a special implement that looks like ivory but is in fact plastic. You would think it was a sort of religious ritual going back to the days of the Druids. In fact draught Guinness was introduced in 1961, prior to which it was only available in bottles.

One reason for the special taste of Irish stout and whiskey is the marvelous quality of Irish water, and this has been the case for many years. Spanish sailors from the Armada fleet who were shipwrecked on the Irish coast in 1588 are said to have so much admired the sweetness of the water that they "could not understand why the Irish should want to drink anything else!"

A word of warning: if you go to a pub and ask for a Guinness or a lager you will automatically be served a pint (about half a liter)—if you want a half-pint, ask for "a glass," or a "half."

Don't Forget to Stand your Round

The Irish are a naturally generous people and, although the "round" system (buying a drink for all in your company) is nothing like as prevalent as it was a generation ago, it is still an important fact of pub culture. If you have accepted a drink from an individual or as part of a round, you should reciprocate. No one will say anything if you do not, but they may not be pleased to see you the following evening. Similarly if you are smoking, you should offer the packet around (again, no comment will be passed if you decide not to; you will simply come across as mildly antisocial).

Licensing laws in Ireland are broadly similar to those in England, and visiting Americans or continental Europeans might regard them as restrictive. Opening hours Monday to Thursday are 10:30 a.m.–11:30 p.m.; Friday and Saturday, 10:30 a.m.–12:30 at night.; and Sunday, 12:30–11:00 p.m., with some city bars having a later licence up to 2.30 a.m. Children (anyone under the age of eighteen) are only allowed in licensed premises if they are with a parent or guardian and may only remain on the premises between the hours of 10:30 a.m. and 9:00 p.m. (10:00 p.m. May to September).

The Irish Don't Drink—That Much!

Nobody works harder to promote an image of wild excess surrounding Irish pub culture than the Irish themselves. However, away from the rush, stress, and hurly-burly of the major cities, the Irish are slow drinkers and can nurse a pint, or a whiskey and water, for a very long time. Then the Irish do not as a rule drink every day, or with their meals. And membership of the influential Catholic temperance movement "The Pioneers" is widespread not just in the Republic but in the North.

A reflection of the changes in Irish society in the last forty years is the way that Irish pubs have been transformed from essentially male-dominated drinking haunts to social centers where both sexes are equally welcome.

There is a wide variety of Irish pubs. In Dublin there are poets' pubs; in some rural areas Gaelic games may be the main topic of conversation; and one Dublin pub has given its name to a school of economics. But above all there are singing pubs and musical pubs where you can hear traditional songs and traditional music, and stand up and sing yourself if you feel so inclined.

So we come to the useful but elusive concept of the *craic*. This is pronounced "crack," but rest easy: the phrase "the *craic* is good," in a certain pub, does not refer to the high quality of the crack cocaine! What it actually means is a bit obscure. Certainly it involves good conversation, but it also implies having a good time when the drink is flowing well, and maybe the music is flowing well. Dancing may even be involved.

Suffice it to say that an Irishman can give no higher praise than that the "*craic* was good." And Irish pubs are the best place to find good *craic*.

THE SPORTING LIFE

With the growth of corporate entertainment in Ireland, business visitors are increasingly likely to find themselves invited to sports events since sports play an important part in national life. And playing golf or going fishing is a good way to meet the Irish in an unselfconscious way.

The Irish love to watch sports. Dublin's main thoroughfares can be deserted when almost everyone is watching a key international match. Similarly the whole country will take a great interest in, and maybe gamble a few euros on, high-profile horse races.

Horse Racing

Involvement in horse racing conveys high status in Ireland, and betting on the outcome is acceptable at all levels of society. Indeed, while the Irish have a love of all forms of sports, they love horses in particular. In the horse-breeding counties of Tipperary, Limerick, and Kildare it is said that only God takes precedence over the horse. That's understandable, since mares from all over the world are brought to Ireland for breeding. The bloodstock industry brings in about a billion euros a year—and the profits are tax-free to the bloodstock owners!

Something of the Irish people's passion for horse racing is conveyed by the fact that there are twenty-eight racecourses in Ireland, almost all in the Republic, attended by more than a million people in the course of a year. The classic flat races, such as the Irish Derby in June, are held at the Curragh in County Kildare. The flat racing season is from mid-March to early November, but National Hunt racing (steeplechasing) over fences, which the Irish claim to have invented, takes place all year. The great classic steeplechase is the Irish Grand National on Easter Monday at Fairyhouse in County Dublin. Probably the most enjoyable event in the racing calendar is the Punchestown festival in March.

Dog Racing

Dog, or greyhound, racing is horse racing's proletarian cousin. It is especially popular in the North and meetings are held at the Drumbo Park Greyhound Stadium in Lambeg, County Antrim. There is even a statue of the legendary Irish greyhound, Master McGrath, in Lurgan, County Armagh.

Soccer

Soccer is not a major sport in the Republic. The Irish team is largely made up of men who play across the water in English or Scottish clubs, and Irish fans all too often prefer to watch these matches on British television rather than go out and support one of the twelve teams in the Irish professional league.

In Northern Ireland soccer is much more popular but has been marred over the years by sectarian tensions, and many Northerners identify with the Glasgow teams where Celtic is regarded as the Catholic team and Rangers the Protestant. Belfast City Airport has been renamed George Best Airport after a famous Northern Irish footballer who, however, spent his life playing for Manchester United in England

Rugby Football

Rugby is sometimes seen as the game of the middle classes, but when Ireland is playing an international match the whole country is glued to its television sets. The Ireland national rugby union team represents the island of Ireland (both the Republic of Ireland and Northern Ireland). The team competes annually in the Six Nations

Championship, which they have won twelve times outright and shared eight times. In March 2015, they won for the second year running.

Gaelic Football and Hurling

The most popular sports in the Republic are the Irish games of Gaelic Football and Hurling. These can attract huge crowds—the highest recorded attendance at an All-Ireland Gaelic Football match was 90,556 in 1961.

Croke Park near Dublin is the headquarters of Gaelic games, though it is also home to international rugby matches. After its recent redevelopment it has a capacity of 82,300, making it the third largest stadium in Europe. It has forty-six hospitality suites containing lavish corporate entertainment facilities. Your Irish hosts are likely to be impressed, and even moved, if you show an interest in Gaelic

sports since they are an essential part of the national ethos. Their revival was a key element in Ireland's rediscovery of itself as a special and unique culture.

Hurling is the true game of the Gael and very ancient—it was played well before St. Patrick brought Christianity to Ireland and was the sport of the heroes of Irish mythology: both Finn McCool and Cúchulainn played it. The modern game has teams

of fifteen players and is fast, skillful, and very dangerous—its original name was *baire boise*, or imitation warfare! It is dangerous because it is played with a heavy "hurley" that looks a little like a hockey stick—though be warned; never compare it with hockey to an Irishman! The blade of the hurley is wide enough for a clever player to balance the ball on it. The goalposts resemble rugby goalposts and points are scored either by hitting the ball over the crossbar or under it. A goal is worth three points.

The revival of Gaelic sports was very much part of the nationalist movement. The Gaelic Athletic Association (GAA) is an amateur sporting association founded in 1884 by the Celtic Revival movement. Its first president was

Dr. T. W. Croke, Catholic bishop of Cashel, after whom Croke Park is named.

Games take place on Sundays—the only free day the Irish agricultural laborer had, and a day when sports were prohibited by the British authorities.

Gaelic Football resembles Hurling in that it has teams of fifteen players, and the same sort of goalposts, where you can score by putting the ball either over or under the crossbar. The ball, which is round like a small soccer ball, can be either kicked or thrown, with one point for putting it over the bar and three for putting it in the net. It is a little like American football, but most resembles Australian football. Today the great event of the Irish sporting calendar is the All-Ireland Gaelic Football final at Croke Park on the third Sunday in September, when the winners are presented with the Sam Maguire cup.

Within six months of the GAA's foundation there were clubs all over Ireland, and today Gaelic Football is played by 250,000 people, Hurling by 100,000, and its female version, "Camogie," by 50,000 women.

The atmosphere at an intercounty match is always one of good will, and the all-Ireland football final in particular is a marvelous occasion. Everyone is there: bishops, priests, farmers, laborers, shopkeepers, and corner boys. Bands play and the President of Ireland throws in the ball. Spectators warmly applaud good playing by each side, and there is none of the hostility between opposing supporters that can make English football matches so disagreeable.

Dress Codes

The casual visitor need not worry unduly about dress at sports events, but the recipients of hospitality should dress fairly formally. A suit or sports jacket, with stout shoes such as brogues would be appropriate for men, while women will find they need to dress with a degree of fashion consciousness so as not to be out of place among their Irish counterparts. A major sports event may be tied in with a formal social occasion, such as a ball, where a tuxedo and equivalent dress for women is likely to be a requirement. Invitees should check this point out in advance.

Golf

The number of golf courses is, in relation to the size of population, among the highest in the world—just under four hundred are affiliated with the Golfing Union of Ireland. Golf has become Ireland's single biggest sporting holiday attraction, contributing 1.8 billion euros to the national economy. Courses vary from those where the major international tournaments are held to a small friendly course in the west where you may have to wave goats away from the green.

Other Sports

Other participation sports like tennis and badminton are well catered for. Dress codes for these sports are much the same as in Britain or the USA.

Road Bowling

There is one sport that is unique to two areas—West Cork in the deep south and Antrim in the far north. I came across it while quietly wandering down a country road in County Cork. Suddenly I was horrified to see a vicious-looking steel ball come hurtling toward me. I had discovered Road Bowling. It is played on Sundays when the Irish roads are even quieter than usual. Intercounty games take place, but they have to be between Cork and Antrim, so the players have to travel the length of Ireland from Antrim in the Protestant North to Cork, the heartland of the Republican South. Neither the Garda nor the Northern Irish police would dream of arresting these sportsmen for misuse of the public highway!

Fishing

With so much water in and around Ireland, and because Ireland's rivers and lakes are the purest in Europe, Ireland both North and South is something of a paradise for anglers.

The Fisheries Board stocks many lakes with rainbow trout, which are not indigenous to Ireland and will not breed there. The true Irish fish are the salmon and the lovely little brown trout, which have an honored place in Irish culture and myth.

While coarse fishing and sea trout fishing are traditional, sea fishing is a relatively new sport. The warm waters of the Gulf Stream mean that fish such as the shark or the blue fin tuna have a far longer season here than elsewhere at these latitudes.

Poachers Turned Gamekeepers

It is characteristic of Irish morality that where I was staying in Donegal the poaching of salmon was considered perfectly moral—after all, the fishing rights were owned by the local landlord who did not even live in the area. But you had to play fair and use a rod and line; anyone who used a net was an outcast. And as for dropping a small stick of dynamite in the river and killing fish that way—that was virtually a hanging offense.

chapter seven

BUSINESS BRIEFING

THE ECONOMY: EIRE

During the enormous economic boom of the so-called "Celtic Tiger," between 1995 and 2000, the Irish economy expanded at an average rate of 9.4 percent a year thanks to a remarkable transition from an agriculture-based economy to an exporting one grounded on modern technology, pharmaceuticals, and the service industries. But this was followed by a property price bubble. It burst in 2007–8 when the American and European economies went into

crisis. The Irish government badly mishandled the collapse and Irish banks lost something like a 100 billion euros. By 2010 the deficit was 132 percent of GDP (see below), the highest in the history of the Eurozone. However, thanks to the combination of the EU/IMF bailout and government prudence—spending cuts and tax hikes between 2008 and 2013 cost every Irish citizen about €6,500, and average income fell 20 percent—Ireland got back on track by 2013. In March 2013 Ireland regained lending access to financial markets and in December it concluded its bailout program on time.

Despite still suffering from the legacy of the crash in the form of a colossal national debt costing an estimated €8.25 billion a year, the Irish economy is thriving. In 2014 it grew by 4.8 percent. The UK was the main export market, accounting for 36 percent of total exports (up by 9 percent from 2013), the USA and Canada accounted for 13 percent of exports (up 16 percent), while much of the remainder went to Germany, the Netherlands, and France. For the first quarter of 2015, exports increased by €3,704 million (up 17 percent) to €24,958 million compared with the first quarter of 2014.

The Republic's GDP

The GDP (Gross Domestic Product) is the monetary value of all the finished goods and services produced within a country's borders, usually calculated on an annual basis. The main source of income and employment in Eire is the service industry. In the most recent figures available, Irish GDP was made up of: services 70.4 percent; industry 28 percent plus; and agriculture 1.6 percent. Similarly the service industries employed most of the labor force, with industry having about a fifth, and just less than a tenth working in agriculture. Among the service industries one of the biggest contributors to

the economy is tourism. Nearly seven and a half million people visited Ireland in 2014—more than one and a half times the country's population. Tourism employs 200,000 people and each year generates €5bn (about 4 percent of GNP).

The Economy Today

There are two distinct export sectors: the traditional, Irish-owned sector; and a newer sector mostly developed with foreign capital based on high-tech production and services.

The indigenous sector is mainly agriculture, forestry, and fishing. When food processing and marketing are included, the agri-food sector accounts for almost 10 percent of employment and nearly 9 percent of Ireland's exports—among them dairy products and baby food exported to China. Additionally recent major discoveries of base metal deposits, including the giant ore deposit at Tara Mine, have made Ireland the largest zinc producer in Europe and the second largest producer of lead.

The technical sector is dominated by multinationals: about forty American firms account for two-thirds of total headline exports, largely because Ireland is the world's most profitable country for US corporations, with a corporation tax rate of 12.5 percent. The Republic is one of the world's largest exporters of pharmaceuticals, medical devices, and computer related goods and services, both hardware and software. According to the Irish Exporters Association the biggest exporters are Google (€17 bn), Microsoft (€15 bn), and Johnson and Johnson (€10.5 bn), while Pfizer (€5 bn) supplies half the world's patented Viagra from plants near Cork.

As a mark of international confidence: at the time of writing the Irish treasury can borrow for two years at an interest rate of 0.016 percent, lower than the rate for Sweden, France, Britain, or the USA.

THE ECONOMY: NORTHERN IRELAND

The largest single occupation is farming: proportionately more cereals are grown than in the Republic, but livestock and dairy products still predominate, and potatoes are also important.

As in the South, most farmers own their farms. Agriculture in Northern Ireland is heavily mechanized, thanks to high labor costs and heavy capital investment, both from private investors and the European Union's Common Agricultural Policy.

The output figures for the local production sector showed a 3.8 percent increase in 2014 compared to the previous year, driven by the manufacturing sector (4.6 percent). Engineering and allied industries were the main areas of growth: 11.5 percent, with basic and fabricated metal products growing 16 percent. Heavy industry tends to be based around Belfast, but Derry and some towns also have industrial areas. Machinery and equipment manufacturing, food processing, and electronics manufacturing are the chief industries; aerospace and paper and furniture-making are also significant.

Today's generation has seen a dramatic shift in manufacturing priorities, with the decline of two formerly dominant industries: textiles and shipbuilding. Harland and Wolff in Belfast (which built the *Titanic* and in the 1940s employed over 35,000 men) slashed their workforce to little more than 100 in 2014, and there is little prospect of any more vessels ever being commissioned. Service industries predominate and the public sector in particular still accounts for a much higher proportion of the workforce than elsewhere in the UK. Above all, Northern Ireland remains heavily dependent on British government subsidies, which total about 20 percent of its GDP.

INTERNATIONALISM

As the Americans, British, and Germans are the largest investors in Ireland, visiting business people should find that dealing with their Irish counterparts in the foreign-funded areas of the economy is not fundamentally different from elsewhere. The workforce is young, computer literate, and professional. Even in the traditional industries, where the approach might seem more relaxed, the law of the bottom line applies as ruthlessly as anywhere else, especially since all sectors of the economy have had to survive the collapse of the "Celtic Tiger."

BUSINESS ETIQUETTE

Even though multinationals dominate business old habits die hard and Irish men and women still tend to dress reasonably formally for meetings— being too casual can give a bad impression, as can being over familiar in manner. Even so, the human touch remains vital. People shake hands on meeting and departure, eye contact is expected, and the old rural tradition of indirectness still survives. It is normal to exchange a few pleasantries before getting down to business, since establishing a warm relationship is considered important. An unassuming courteousness is appreciated, though excessive politeness, especially to a boss, is frowned on—as is excessive praise.

Aggressive sales techniques are rarely appreciated, especially in country areas. Take things slowly and allow your professional relationship to develop as your Irish counterpart comes to know and trust you. The use of first names is standard practice. Exchanging business cards is not routine, so a request for a card can be a sign of genuine interest.

WOMEN IN BUSINESS

The majority of working women in Ireland work in business and there is no legal discrimination at any level, but some men still assume women are secretaries or personal assistants, so if you are the boss or a senior executive make your position clear discreetly but clearly.

MANAGEMENT STYLE

In smaller businesses the boss is often the key decision-maker and authority figure; but this may be masked by an atmosphere of informal communication in which instructions are often presented in the form of polite requests. These businesses tend to be conservative, especially when it comes to making decisions. As in the UK there is a tendency for decision-making to be on an "ad hoc" short-term basis, in preference to long-term planning.

MEETINGS, NEGOTIATIONS, AND COMMUNICATION

Meetings are generally welcoming, warm, and friendly. A "down-to-earth" approach is appreciated. Agendas are not inviolate, and there is a certain resistance to structure and routine. Ideas are as important as facts, so by all means be imaginative—Irish businesses embrace creativity and are always looking for new ways to approach problems and tasks. But a caveat: such daring is not always followed up. The way things are done can be regarded as just as important as getting a result.

Some Dos and Don'ts

Do not try to shortcut established processes—go with them, sell your ideas gently—however much you may know you are right. Justify what you say in an objective, reasonable way.

Do not precipitate confrontations. Be tactful: it pays to start from a position of apparent agreement and compliance. Open dissent is rare so be prepared to read between the lines; responses can be cryptic. A period of silence in conversation is likely to signal problems.

In presenting your case, an informal, conversational style usually works best. The quality and style of your language will be significant, and humor, anecdotes, and jokes are appreciated—but avoid sarcasm.

Also avoid too much technical language, too many visual aids, and the like. To prove points rely on simple practical facts and verbal fluency.

Do not be fooled by any apparent dreaminess; the Irish are cunning businessmen.

"The Irish are a very spiritual people, and the longer it takes you to pay them the more spiritual they become."
Conor Cruise O'Brien

There are no words for "yes" and "no" in true Gaelic, and perhaps this is why the Irish do not like to say "yes" or "no" outright. Be prepared for noncommittal answers ". . . maybe, perhaps . . ." It is not a good idea to force decisions, as this may damage relationships.

TEAMS AND TEAMWORK

In larger businesses team members work cooperatively, combining their skills, and decisions are reached by consultation. The leader's job is to embody the collective will—and feeling insufficiently consulted is a common cause of disagreement. Team members expect to be consulted and to influence the outcome. However, be wary—when things go wrong there can be a tendency to blame individuals rather than accept collective responsibility.

It is not a good idea to put pressure on people: it tends to have the reverse effect and even slow things down.

BUSINESS ENTERTAINING

Entertaining and socializing are very much part of business life, and are generally informal in style: visitors are as likely to be invited to lunch in a pub or in the company canteen as in a restaurant. Lunch is usually taken at 12:30 or 1:00 p.m.

The ability to relax and enjoy whatever entertainment is provided is important. Join in and treat your hosts as friends: ostentatious self-importance will be considered insulting. A visiting businessman may well be taken to a nightclub after dinner where the revelry can continue into the small hours. Pubs where music is performed, especially traditional music, are a common feature of Irish life, and visitors are often taken along.

It is quite likely that you and your spouse will be invited to your host's home, usually at about 7:30 or 8:00 p.m. If you are, take a small present for the hostess: wine or chocolates. Dress is usually informal but not overly casual. It is normal to return hospitality.

Relax with a Song!

Shyness or reticence is understood, but the visitor who, when invited, can launch into a song or a ballad from their own culture will certainly be appreciated. And it will help in establishing a relaxed personal relationship with your Irish hosts that will definitely be advantageous when it comes to business negotiations.

Appointments

Despite the famous Irish casualness about time, the old *laissez-faire* attitudes are being squeezed out of Irish economic life. If your Irish counterparts are serious about doing business with you they will be punctual and will expect the same from you.

The English tend not to confirm business appointments made by telephone, but in Ireland it is as well to follow up by fax, letter, or e-mail, and to make a final confirmation by telephone the day before meeting.

Unless your host specifies casual dress, wear a suit for a dinner party. Entry to some nightclubs will be facilitated by wearing a jacket and tie. Some upmarket restaurants may expect similar attire.

BUSINESS AND SHOPPING HOURS

Most businesses in Ireland, both North and South, operate a forty-hour, five-day week.

Shops are generally open from 9:00 or 9:30 a.m. to 5:30 or 6:00 p.m., Monday to Saturday, but in the smaller towns some still close for at least an hour at lunchtime and on one afternoon each week, usually Wednesday or Thursday.

However, in the cities especially, nowadays there are late-opening minisupermarkets catering for people who operate outside conventional working hours, and Sunday opening is becoming reasonably common in the Republic, less so in Northern Ireland. In the North, Sunday trading rules allow small shops to choose their own Sunday opening hours but large shops may only open between 1:00 p.m. and 6:00 p.m.

BANKING AND CREDIT/DEBIT CARDS

Banks hours across Ireland are generally from 9:00 a.m. to 4:00 p.m., Monday to Friday, though some remain open until 4:30 p.m. or 5:00 p.m. Most close at weekends and public holidays, though Saturday opening is becoming more common. But there are plenty of ATM machines and Visa, MasterCard/Eurocard are usually accepted at hotels, gas stations, and payphones. American Express (AmEx) is accepted, but not nearly as readily as in the US. Diners Club, JCB, and Discover are generally not accepted. Debit cards without a Maestro, Visa Debit, or MasterCard logo are not accepted.

chapter eight

COMMUNICATING

A LOVE OF LANGUAGE

The gift of the "blarney" is generally supposed
to represent the archetypical Irishman's ability to
charm, and there is some truth in the stereotype.
Verbal fluency is valued in Ireland. It is what
"the *craic*" is all about, and the unbroken line
of outstanding Irish playwrights from the
eighteenth century onward bears witness to
the Irish joy in words and discourse.

THE IMPORTANCE OF
UNDERSTATEMENT

While picturesque phrases and colorful images
may abound, this is counterbalanced by gently
ironic understatement. Somebody who is
terminally ill might be said to be looking "a bit
shook." If someone suggests a "gargle" they
mean going for a drink.

   This indirectness often represents a
delicate linguistic camouflage under which
uncomfortable truths can be hinted at, or
propositions advanced, with minimal loss of

face if rejected. It is important in doing business, especially in rural areas, to be tuned in to these subtleties.

At a deeper level, beneath the general bonhomie, the Irish are reticent about exposing their innermost feelings. Not as formal as the English in personal relationships, the Irish are nevertheless unlikely to bare their souls to anybody other than close friends or family.

Learn Patience

The Irish love of conversation means it can be a fine test of one's patience to stand in, say, a supermarket line while the checkout girl chatters to the customer ahead of you about their respective families. Look on it as good training for doing business with an Irish countryman!

WATCH OUT FOR GOSSIP

The small size of Ireland means everybody knows (or thinks they know) everybody else's business. Gossip travels fast. The other side of the coin is that everyone is keen to preserve their privacy. Consequently there often emerges a wonderful contradiction whereby, in trying to preserve their own privacy, people cheerfully gossip about others in order to keep the limelight off themselves.

ACCENT AND IDIOM

Despite its small population, there is a lot of regional variation in Ireland, in both accent and phrasing. Dublin people have a famous nasal twang, while the Cork accent is notoriously singsong, and the western soft and gentle. The harsher Northern accent can sound more like Scots, especially in Belfast City.

Although few Irish people speak Gaelic fluently, many Irish turns of phrase derive from Gaelic usage. Irish has a tense called "the present habitual" and you might hear something like "There does be a meeting of the board every Tuesday," but anyone proficient in English should have little difficulty in understanding what is meant.

Beware of Stereotypes

Cheery Hollywood stereotypes who utter phrases like "top of the morning" (which nobody actually says in Ireland), can be dangerously misleading. In particular visitors who put on fake Irish accents are not appreciated. And, whatever may be the case in the United States, in Ireland a *shillelagh* is not a blackthorn walking stick but a vicious cudgel sometimes kept behind bars to deal with awkward customers!

THE MEDIA
Irish Newspapers
Ireland is well provided with newspapers, which have a good mix of national and international news. The *Irish Times*, regarded as the flagship quality daily (though the *Irish Independent* has a larger circulation), is transmitted daily on the Internet. British newspapers are available throughout Ireland from early on the day of issue.

Partisan Reporting
Belfast papers can be quite sectarian in their reporting. Supposedly when a drunk was run over on the train track a Republican newspaper was said to have run the headline "Catholic Killed by Government Train!" Some British tabloids print Irish editions, and during the Troubles anti-Irish English headlines frequently became rather different in these editions!

TV and Radio

The digital terrestrial television service Saorview became the main source of broadcast television when analog transmissions ended in 2012. Eire's publicly-funded TV and radio network, RTE (*Radio Telefis Eirann*: "RAD-io TEL-e-FEES AIR-un"), has two English-language TV channels, RTE1 and Network 2, and an Irish-language channel, TG4. All carry commercials, but there is also an independent commercial station, TV3.

The three English-language RTE radio networks are Radio 1, Radio 2, and the classical music station Lyric FM; plus Radio Ireland, the Irish-language *Radio na Gaeltachta*, and numerous local stations.

BBC radio and TV are generally easily obtainable, and digital satellite transmissions from Sky Ireland, Saorsat, and several European satellite services are also available, as is cable .

Northern Ireland has the BBC radio and TV channels plus the commercial Ulster Television,

over half of whose viewers are in the Republic.
There are a number of local radio stations.

COMMUNICATING AND GETTING AROUND

Telephone

The Irish telecommunications system is
100 percent digital, and the cell phone
network serves more than 95 percent
of the population, North and South.
Visiting businesspeople should have
no difficulty with laptops or cell
phones (provided they are designed
for international use). Americans should
be aware that local calls are charged. There
are a number of Internet providers.

Unfortunately, because they are used to
friendly chatter on the telephone, older Irish
people are not good with voice mail—if the
person they are calling is not there they often
simply hang up!

To dial out from Eire use the 00 code. For
example to dial the UK (including Northern
Ireland) dial 0044 plus the area code without the
0 in front—thus the UK number 01632 961084
should be dialled as 0044 1632 961084.

To call Eire from any other country the code
is +353 (00 353 from UK).

The Northern Ireland service is the same as
that of the rest of the UK and calls to the Republic
count as international calls.

Rail and Bus

The Eire Rail network connects the main towns and cities. Lines run from Dublin to Sligo, and Ballina in the north, Westport, Galway, Tralee, and Ennis in the west, and Cork, Rosslare, and Bridgetown in the south. Rail is a fast, cheap, and reliable way of getting around (though not to more remote locations), and there are express trains to Belfast (the "Enterprise" takes two hours). Dublin has its own metropolitan railway, the DART. The bus service, too, can be useful. On Dublin buses the destination *An Lar* (pronounced as written) is the Irish for "city center."

Northern Ireland is poorly served by rail, but from Belfast, as well as "The Enterprise," there is a route to Londonderry and a couple of other shorter routes. And the Province has an efficient and wide-ranging bus network.

Of course the wealthier or those on large expense accounts can get around the island by helicopter or by plane using the regional airports of Donegal, Galway, Kerry, Sligo, Waterford, and Derry.

The Border

The border between the Republic and Northern Ireland is almost invisible. No passport is needed unless you require a visa for Ireland or the UK. If so, you should keep your passport with you.

Roads

The Irish drive on the left as in Britain. Both South and North have higher grade roads called Motorways and marked with an M— those in the South charge a toll for their use.

But generally roads throughout Ireland are reasonable, thanks to major subsidies from the EU, and are delightfully uncluttered—though they are narrower than in the US, and you might be held up by slow agricultural vehicles or even herds of sheep and cattle.

Taxis and Taxi Drivers

Taxis in urban areas operate from ranks or by telephone call: they do not cruise the streets, as in New York or London. Irish taxis can be a means, not only of transport, but of education. For many visitors on their way in from the airport, the taxi driver will be their first encounter with the irreverent, opinionated, garrulous Dubliner. If you wish to sit stiffly, shrouding yourself in executive privilege, he will not mind, but you may be the loser.

Car Rental

Car rental (usually known as "car hire" in Ireland) can be expensive by British or US standards and comparatively few rental cars are automatic. It is best to arrange rental before you arrive.

CONCLUSION

The best thing that visitors to Ireland can do is relax and be themselves. You cannot become Irish by a process of osmosis (though some people try!) and no one is expected to master all the subtleties of the local culture. The foreigner in Ireland has a general dispensation to be different. But this book will have given you some idea of what makes the Irish tick: how they conduct business, how they spend their leisure, what they eat and drink, and, above all, what is so special about Ireland. How a hospitable and creative, small island people have had such an impact on the world, and created a culture and literature of which a nation twenty times their size would be proud. And, of course, how they have been shaped by their geography and their history—and maybe why some of them chose not to go West and seek their fortunes in the USA!

Appendix: Some Famous Irish Americans

Eleven Presidents of the United States had Irish roots:
Andrew Jackson, James K. Polk, James Buchanan, Ulysses S. Grant,
William McKinley, Woodrow Wilson, John Fitzgerald Kennedy,
Richard Milhous Nixon, Ronald Reagan, and Bill Clinton. Even
Barack Obama can claim Irish lineage, though somewhat obscurely,
through his mother's diverse ancestry.

Two signatories of the Declaration of Independence were born
in Ireland: George Taylor and Matthew Thornton.

Other signatories with Irish roots are:
Thomas Lynch, Thomas McLean, George Read, Edward Rutledge,
James Smith, and Charles Carroll, the only Catholic to sign.

Notable Irish-Americans include:
Daniel Boone and Davy Crockett, frontiersmen; Buffalo Bill Cody,
showman; Bat Masterson, gunfighter; John O'Hara, Scott Fitzgerald,
and Eugene O'Neill, writers; Henry Ford, automobile manufacturer;
John Ford, filmmaker; James Cagney, Jackie Gleason, Buster Keaton,
Gene Kelly, Grace Kelly, Bing Crosby, and Gregory Peck, actors;
Stephen Foster, songwriter; Randolph Hearst, newspaper owner;
Ed Murrow, CBS correspondent; John McEnroe, tennis player;
John McCloskey, first American cardinal of the Catholic Church;
and William J. Brennan and Sandra Day O'Connor, Supreme
Court justices.

Further Reading

Behan, Brendan. *After the Wake*. Dublin: The O'Brien Press, 1998.

Cahill, Thomas. *How the Irish Saved Civilization*. New York: Anchor Books, 1995.

Callan, Lou, et al. *Lonely Planet: Ireland*. Melbourne/Oakland/London/Paris: Lonely Planet Publications, 2002.

Connolly, S. J. *The Oxford Companion to Irish History*. Oxford: OUP, 1998.

Dwyer, T. Ryal. *Michael Collins and the Civil War*. Dublin: The Mercier Press, 2012.

Joyce, J. *Ulysses*. New York: Random House, 1934.

Kennedy & Gillispie (eds.). I*reland: Art into History*. Dublin: Townhouse, 1994.

Kinsella, Thomas (ed. and trans.). *The New Oxford Book of Irish Verse*. Oxford: OUP, 2001.

Longley, Michael (ed.) *20th Century Irish Poems*. London: Faber, 2002.

McGahern, John. *The Dark*. London: Faber, 1965.

_____ *That They May Face the Rising Sun*. London: Faber, 2001.

Montague, John (ed.). *The Faber Book of Irish Verse*. London: Faber, 1974.

Moody, T. W. & Martin, F. X. *The Course of Irish History*. Dublin: Mercier Press, 1994.

O'Brien, Flann. *The Third Policeman*. New York: New American Library, 1986.

_____ *At Swim-two-birds*. Penguin Modern Classics, 1939.

Synge, J. M. *The Aran Islands*. Oxford: OUP, 1990.

Vallely, Fintan. *Companion to Irish Traditional Music*. Cork: Cork University Press, 1998.

Yeats, W. B. *Poems, Selected by Seamus Heaney*. London: Faber, 2002.

Wallis Paul et al. The Rough Guide to Ireland London: Rough Guides, 2011

Wallis Paul et al. The Rough Guide to Ireland London: Rough Guides, 2011

Wallis, Paul, et al. *The Rough Guide to Ireland*. London: Rough Guides, 2011.

Web Sites

Discover Ireland: The official Irish Tourist board.
www.discoverireland.ie/Tourism_Ireland

IDA Ireland is the government agency responsible for industrial development in Ireland.
www.idaireland.com/

Invest NI: Northern Ireland Government Development Agency.
www.investni.com

Discover Northern Ireland The official Northern Irish Tourist board.
www.discovernorthernireland.com.

Trip Advisor.
http://www.tripadvisor.co.uk/Travel-g186591-c71046/Ireland:Airports.And.Ferry. Services.html

Index